Jossey-Bass Teacher

Jossey-Bass Teacher provides educators with practical knowledge and tools to create a positive and lifelong impact on student learning. We offer classroom-tested and research-based teaching resources for a variety of grade levels and subject areas. Whether you are an aspiring, new, or veteran teacher, we want to help you make every teaching day your best.

From ready-to-use classroom activities to the latest teaching framework, our value-packed books provide insightful, practical, and comprehensive materials on the topics that matter most to K–12 teachers. We hope to become your trusted source for the best ideas from the most experienced and respected experts in the field.

D0890983

The Field Guide to Counseling Toward Solutions

The Solution-Focused School

Linda Metcalf

JOSSEY-BASS
A Wiley Imprint
www.josseybass.com

Published by Jossey-Bass
A Wiley Imprint
989 Market Street, San Francisco, CA 94103-1741—www.josseybass.com

Jossey-Bass books and products are available through most bookstores. To contact Jossey-Bass directly call our Customer Care Department within the U.S. at 800-956-7739, outside the U.S. at 317-572-3986, or fax 317-572-4002.

Jossey-Bass also publishes its books in a variety of electronic formats. Some content that appears in print may not be available in electronic books.

ISBN: 9780787998073

Printed in the United States of America

FIRST EDITION

HB Printing   10 9 8 7 6 5 4 3 2 1
PB Printing   10 9 8 7 6 5 4 3 2 1

About This Book

Welcome to a solution-focused field guide that will take you through the hallways, classrooms, and meeting rooms of your school and help you transform the climate into one where parents, staff, and students react more positively and collaboratively. Inside this book are tips for integrating and implementing the solution-focused approach with parents, teachers, teams, and special educators, given in a step-by-step format that makes learning the model easy.

The book begins with a survey for you to take that will help you determine whether your school is steeped in problem talk or flourishing with solution talk. It then takes you through the workings of a typical school and shows you how to implement ideas that keep students, teachers, and parents on track and help them to realize their potential. It does all of this in an informative, simple, and practical manner with reproducible sheets that simplify your job by telling you what to say and write. This book also provides all of the tools you need to present staff development ideas that are tailored specifically to your school's grade levels.

The solutions for your school have arrived. Go forth, and change its climate!

Dedicated to school counselors, their students, and staff members.
Make the days exceptional!

About the Author

Linda Metcalf, Ph.D., is a former middle school teacher, a certified school counselor, a licensed marriage and family therapist, and a licensed professional counselor. She has been an elementary school counselor, secondary school counselor, and a safe and drug-free coordinator in public schools. She is an associate professor and the director of school counseling at Texas Wesleyan University in the Department of Education and lives in Arlington, Texas, where she works extensively with school systems as a consultant in solution-focused therapy and with children, adolescents, and families. She is the author of several books on the solution-focused approach and its use by parents, teachers, and groups. She has been a frequent presenter at the Texas Association for School Counselors; the Texas Association for Marriage and Family Therapists; the American Association for Marriage and Family Therapy, of which she is a national board member; and the American School Counselor Association. She has presented over two hundred workshops throughout the United States and Canada, in addition to workshops in Australia, Japan, Singapore, Norway, Scotland, Germany, and England.

Acknowledgments

This book is and always will be a work in progress. That's because wherever you go, wherever you look, there will always be the need for a new idea in a school. For the past twelve years, I have had the luxury of meeting school counselors who are hungry for a new approach. Their questions and situations kept me searching to find new ways to apply the solution-focused approach in a variety of settings. Many of those inquiries that left me feeling stuck emerged later in programs such as those set forth by Davenport Community Schools. To Betty Long of Davenport Community Schools and James O'Hare, of the Mississippi Bend Area Education Agency, I send my warmest appreciation for what you do each day with students and staff. I learned alongside you how to motivate and implement the solution-focused approach into not only the process of special education referrals but in your high schools and alternative school. Your work was groundbreaking.

Thanks to Margie McAneny, who promoted my idea of a field guide to counseling toward solutions and helped me to achieve what I feel is the most practical application yet to creating a solution-focused school environment. I appreciated your perseverance and assistance as I "did surgery" on the original *Counseling Toward Solutions*, revising it and writing this companion guide.

To Chris Hooker, a new, talented therapist who took a wraparound facilitator position and transformed it into a solution-focused role with grand success, you are on your way to being a great therapist. My appreciation goes as well to Nicole Shannon, a therapist whose work with one child taught her that she needed only to try new language to entice a mom into a better relationship with her daughter. Terry Walkup, you have my admiration for all you do with my favorite group: adolescents. Thank you for inspiring me to always name solution-focused groups accordingly to set the atmosphere for solutions rather than problems. To Anita McNew, a therapist who learned firsthand how the solution-focused process can aid parents in day-to-day drudgeries, thank you for sharing your story of success.

Thanks to the unending support and motivation that Garza Gonzales High School in Austin, Texas, gives its staff and students. Your school is a model for all to see. I appreciate how you, along with Cynthia Franklin and Insoo Berg, have created a culture where students want to be competent.

Finally, I would like to acknowledge my family's support while writing yet another book and our two golden retrievers, Rex 1 and Rex 2, who snored alongside my desk. You have proven to me that by living life with a solution-focused lens, everything can be a little bit rosier.

Contents

About This Book   v

About the Author   vii

Acknowledgments   ix

Preface   xiii

1 Setting the Stage for Success   1

2 Training Staff to Become Solution Focused   13

3 Working Together with Teams, Teachers, and Parents   43

4 Stopping the Special Education Referrals Creatively   53

5 Combining Your Resources: Solution-Focused Support Groups   71

6 The Solution-Focused School   97

Bibliography and References   119

Index   121

Preface

If you are not part of the solution, you are part of the problem.

—Eldridge Cleaver

Solution-focused therapy has taken the mental health field by storm. The model has been used effectively with a variety of mental health issues affecting individuals and families. Instead of trying to understand the root of the problem, the model focuses on the times when the problem occurs less frequently, making it a perfect fit for school counselors, teachers, and administrators who have little time to understand why these problems crop up. By identifying the specific interactions, behaviors, and thinking that help the problem to occur less often, students, teachers, and parents realize that they can figure out their own solutions. The school counselor's job then becomes one of facilitating change within the school client by identifying those times, situations, and context when the problem occurs less often. The conversations become focused on instilling hope through identifying exceptions, that is, those times when the problem occurs less, rather than dwelling on problems themselves.

This book aims to add solution-focused skills to school counselors' toolboxes so that they can reach more school clients, doing so more efficiently and in less time, and thereby have less stressful days. By using solution-focused therapy approaches and applying them to typical school situations, school counselors everywhere can begin to change the climate at their school, lessening resistance among students, parents, and staff and rekindling the climate that schools were originally meant to have: a positive one, full of hope for their students.

This book blends a narrative therapy approach with the solution-focused approach so that students with historical labels identifying them as "problems" can break free from such categorical traps and rebuild a new story with their teachers, parents, and staff members. Narrative therapy teaches that school clients get stuck in their lives when the stories of their lives, often written by many "coauthors" (parents, family history, school staff, and peers) take over. These characters and situations become the only story that the school client knows.

For example, in a problem-focused school, a child diagnosed with attention deficit disorder becomes a child who knows he is distractible and his teachers know he is distractible, so they believe he can't possibly concentrate ever. This belief ties everyone's hands and keeps school clients from trying anything new. Or a single parent who has been told she is not giving her child enough help at night with homework sees herself as an unsuccessful parent, and she responds defensively and blames the school. These school clients are limited by their perceptions of themselves.

Narrative therapy offers a different perception, and by changing the perception, behaviors change as well.

As you read this book, go on a mental vacation and put aside your stress, worries, and problem-focused approaches. The chapters are arranged in a sequence of how the program can be implemented best, so think of the program as a work in progress. Envision how a solution-focused approach can transform your faculty, students, and parents and your job instead of how difficult it might be to begin. Realize that each year, your school has probably implemented some new programming, changed a few processes, and adopted new textbooks. Your school clients know how to deal with change. And as you think about it, there are probably people in your school who deal with change in ways that could motivate others to follow along. These people will become your cohorts. See this program as one more opportunity to try something new. And with that confidence, let's do it!

Linda Metcalf

The Field Guide to Counseling Toward Solutions

Chapter One

Setting the Stage for Success

*You cannot solve a problem with the same
kind of thinking that created it.*

—Albert Einstein

Imagine for a moment how different the job of an educator would be in a solution-focused school rather than a problem-focused school. Imagine going to work each day knowing that the following occurrences were routine:

- Staff meetings focus on priority school goals, and all members of the staff strategize together on the steps to accomplish them.

- Students become part of the solution for their own academic or behavior issues by identifying times when they are slightly more successful. By identifying their own solutions, students are more likely to follow through with tasks to change their behavior and academic status.

- Parents are more prone to work with the school regarding their child's education because the school counselor and administrator use the parent as a consultant rather than tell the parents what is wrong with their child.

- Teachers see themselves and their students as competent individuals and deal with challenges in the classroom on their own, using solution-focused conversations that result in respect between both parties.

- The community sees the school as a place where the atmosphere is supportive of both parent and student ideas and flexible enough to think creatively for a variety of student needs.

- A mentor program develops the at-risk student into a promising student by pairing the student with a faculty mentor who aims to build a new relationship with the student.

Any school can achieve these outcomes.

To begin using the ideas in this field guide, a change in mind-set is necessary: school staff must make a shift in their thinking from problem focus to solution focus. Chapter Two provides school counselors and administrators with ample information on training the school staff effectively. But first this chapter serves as an assessment tool to help you measure whether your school is problem focused or solution focused.

Evaluate Your School First

On a scale of 1 to 10, with 1 being problem focused and 10 being solution focused, where would you place your school? The School Strategies Survey is designed to help measure how solution focused your school is at this time. It will be helpful to take the survey as a school counselor and randomly give it to teachers and administrators and compare their responses. Many of the answers will not be surprising; some may be. At the end of the survey, tally up the scores, and compare your score with those of others who have taken the survey. Use the results to help persuade your administrator that it's time for a change in regard to how problems are addressed. Let the survey "do the talking" in regard to how collaborative and solution focused your school staff really is. It's time to take a hard look at things and see if they are working. If they are not, it's time for a solution-focused approach.

School Strategies Survey

Circle the answers that show how incidents are *currently* handled at your school.

------

1. When a teacher is upset with a student's disrespectful attitude toward another student, first, the teacher:

   a. Sends the offending student or students to the administrator.

   b. Scolds the offending student and tells the student to reread the class rules.

   c. Talks to both students, relaying concern, and then brainstorms with the students ways to get things to work better between them in the classroom.

   d. Calls the offending student's parent to let the parent know what is happening and threatens that the student may not make it through school with this attitude.

2. When a student begins to have difficulty learning a new concept, the teacher takes the following action first:

   a. Asks the student what the problem is and tells the student that in order to pass the class, he or she must try harder.

   b. Waits to see if the student improves on his or her own.

   c. Tries other methods to reach the student and checks with the student's other teachers to learn about their success with him or her.

   d. Calls the student's parents, describes the problem, and tells them that they are responsible for changing the student's behavior.

3. When a student shows unacceptable behaviors, the teacher takes the following action first:

   a. Gives the same consequences consistently even if the consequences do not work.

   b. Contacts the parents and has a parent conference to get home support.

   c. Talks to the student privately in a respectful manner, tells the student that the behavior is unacceptable, and together they create an agreed-on plan designed to stop the behaviors.

   d. Informs the parents of the consequences if the behavior continues.

4. When a parent conference is held regarding a student's poor academic performance, the following occurs the most often:

   a. The teacher tells the parent that the school has done all that can be done, and now the student must put forth effort.

School Strategies Survey (cont.)

    b. The student is not present, and the teacher tells the parents about the problems that the student is having in school.

    c. The teacher asks the parent to look at past teachers and classes where the student was successful and builds interventions with the parent based on those ideas.

    d. The teacher discusses tutoring options for the student.

5. When a teacher meets with an administrator to discuss a student or parent he or she is struggling with, the administrator first tells the teacher to:

    a. Call the parents and tell them what the problems are and what the consequences will be if the problems are not solved soon.

    b. Refer the student to the school counselor for testing.

    c. Deal with the issue initially and think how she was able to deal with challenging students in the past. The administrator compliments the teacher by saying that he knows she is competent and can find some answers. When she does, she is to let him know as a follow-up.

    d. Set up a behavioral plan and to report after six weeks.

6. In February, a student is identified by his teacher as having difficulties in math. Until February, the student's math grades were in the 80s. The student also appears very sleepy in the morning. If you were an administrator, what would you suggest the teacher do first?

    a. Speak to the boy and let him know what is expected of him during the school year, listing consequences for sleeping in class.

    b. Contact the parent and find out if something is happening at home to cause the problem.

    c. Speak with other teachers regarding the student's performance in their classes before February and then talk to the student about what might need to happen to get back on track in math.

    d. Suggest that the student be placed on a behavioral plan with the counselor.

7. A student comes to school upset and storms into her first class, slams down her books on the desk, and glares at the teacher. When the teacher asks her to quiet down, she talks back disrespectfully. Which dialogue is more likely to happen in your school first?

    a. "Charlotte, it looks as if you need to reread the classroom rules on the bulletin board. Coming in as you did is not appropriate, and you have just lost five points on your citizenship grade."

    b. "Charlotte, you need to go into the hall because your behavior this morning is disturbing other students, and it is not acceptable."

School Strategies Survey (cont.)

   c. "Class, begin reading silently. Charlotte, come out into the hallway with me, please. (In the hall) It seems that you are having a tough morning. I enjoy your company in class and know that others are concerned about you. What can I do to help you settle into the class routine this morning?"

   d. "Charlotte, it looks as if you need to see the counselor. Here is your pass."

8. A parent calls a teacher and requests a conference to talk about his son's science grade, which had been declining. At the conference, a teacher in your school is likely to do which of the following?

   a. Tell the father that the son belongs in a lower science class since he obviously is not interested in school work.

   b. Provide the father the course requirements and tell him which assignments his son has not completed, citing his poor performance on incomplete work and inattentiveness in class.

   c. Invite the father and the son to attend the conference. He would then tell the father how glad he was that he called because during the beginning of the year, his son was a top student. The teacher would then listen to the father and focus on the grades that were passing, suggesting that the son must have done something different during those times. The teacher would next ask the son what was different. As the conference ends, the teacher would ask what he could do to help.

   d. Tell the father about tutoring possibilities outside school.

9. A teacher becomes concerned about a student who she thinks has a lot of academic potential but does not do assignments. She calls his home and leaves many messages that are never returned. Frustrated, she talks to her team. Which advice that follows would the team give first?

   a. Don't try so hard. Without parental support, there is only so much that a teacher can do. Stop trying harder than the student.

   b. Continue calling the family, and visit the home if necessary.

   c. After brainstorming how to assist the student, the team members advise bringing the student into the meeting and asking how the team can help. The teacher then feels supported by her colleagues and decides to try some new ways of reaching the student based on what the student discussed in the meeting. After a few weeks, the team will meet again with the student.

   d. Refer the student to the counselor to see if she can figure out what can be done with community resources.

10. A student has great difficulty sitting in his seat. He is a good student but tends to fidget so much that he distracts the other students. He is polite and respectful but absolutely cannot control his tapping pencil and rattling papers. In response to numerous requests by the teacher to be quiet in class, the teacher decides to try the following first:

School Strategies Survey (cont.)

a. Send the student to the administrator for detention since the student "refuses" to comply with classroom rules and be quiet.

b. Call the parents and suggest that they consult a physician about giving him medication for an attention disorder.

c. Ask the student how he or she (the teacher) can help with the "excess energy" that seems to control his every move in class. When the student suggests doing errands for the teacher after his work is completed, the teacher agrees.

d. Talk to the student and tell him that life will be hard if he cannot learn to control his attention deficit disorder. Bosses will not tolerate such defiance.

Score: List the number of responses to the following letters:

a _____

b _____

c _____

d _____

After you collect the surveys from others, add up the scores together and apply your results to the following guidelines:

a = If the majority of the numbers are in this category, your school staff are very problem focused.

b = If the majority of the numbers are in this category, your staff are problem focused and try to tell students how to solve their problems in a noncollaborative manner.

c = If the majority of the numbers are in this category, congratulations! Your staff are likely to be open to the solution-focused approach.

d = If the majority of the numbers are in this category, your staff tend to take the least responsible route to helping the students.

What to Do Next

School surveys that have higher scores in a, b, and d will benefit from every exercise suggested in Chapter Two. The staff will also need to hear from the principal how supportive the administration is in achieving a solution-focused atmosphere in your school. But how do you get the administrator on board?

It may be helpful to show the administrator the resource companion to this field guide, *Counseling Toward Solutions*, and discuss the following ideas that will help teachers, parents, and the administrator to become more solution focused:

- The program will serve everyone and will promote positive self-esteem and competency among students, parents, and school staff.

- The program will offer teachers alternative ways of reaching at-risk students, lessening the load on vice principals and increasing capacity in teachers.

- The program will assist teachers in dealing with classroom management more effectively by creating new relationships with students.

- Students will become partners in their educational process rather than receivers of cookie-cutter intervention, making them more responsible and motivated.

- The program may lessen the dependence of teachers on the school counselor and free up the school counselor to provide more programming.

You may want to add other options that your school would like to promote once it begins the solution-focused school program. Additional ideas for groups, staff meetings, parent conferences, and teams are just a few that will benefit from becoming solution focused at your school.

To be even more prepared to get administrative support, consider using the Buy-In Questions worksheet with the administrator at your school. As you read through the questions, notice that they are solution focused. Just by asking them of your administrator, you can see how the process can work.

Buy-In Questions

1. If you had your way, what would you want to achieve in the next school year?

_____

_____

What else?

_____

_____

What else?

_____

_____

2. Let's say that in the near future, your ideas begin to happen. What would be different? What difference would that make for you, your teachers, and your students? If the administrator says your ideas won't happen or seems negative, ask him or her to brainstorm briefly.

_____

_____

_____

_____

On a scale of 1 to 10, with 10 meaning you have achieved each of these goals and 1 meaning you haven't even approached it yet, where would you put yourself and the school? _____

Where would you like to be in the next few months? _____

Ending: I would like to tell you about a program that might begin to achieve what we are talking about. I am willing to lead the program if you will endorse it. I also have a survey that I gave a few colleagues. Here are the results. Can I leave you some information and check back next week?

Imagine the answers that you will get! By preparing in advance to ask these questions, you can try out the model with the administrator. The questions also embrace the vision of the administrator, giving you a better opportunity to present the school program. While *buy-in* is a business term, it is also a core component of the solution-focused approach because it goes where the school client is and therefore motivates him or her to try something new. And no matter what the goals and vision of the administrator are, the school program can begin addressing it. Suppose the school administrator tells you that her vision is a new school building. Go with it! Become the solution-focused school counselor. Here's how that dialogue might go:

COUNSELOR: What a great idea. What would that do for you, the students, and the teachers?

ADMINISTRATOR: We would be able to be state of the art, and the cracking ceilings and old computers would be history.

COUNSELOR: How would that make a difference?

ADMINISTRATOR: Our students could learn more technology, feel more comfortable, and be ready for the workplace in a few years, and our teachers could try new teaching methods.

COUNSELOR: What else?

ADMINISTRATOR: We could be more creative by having new equipment. I think it would excite the teachers and let them know the district is investing in education.

COUNSELOR: And when your teachers are more creative, what would you see them doing?

ADMINISTRATOR: Trying out new projects with the students.

COUNSELOR: And when your teachers know that the district is investing in education, what would that do?

ADMINISTRATOR: It might improve their morale. It might make them think they were important, and their attitudes would be different—more positive.

COUNSELOR: These are terrific ideas. What have you done before with this staff or even other staff members that helped them to be more positive and creative?

This dialogue is not that far off from what could happen as you begin to explore what your administrator sees as a real vision. The key is to ask this question: "How would that make a difference for you?" This question takes a goal that is a bit hard to accomplish because of logistics, finances, and other situations and helps people to go within their vision and see where it realistically could still take them. The means to get to the goal may be different from a brand-new school building, but the alternative means that are generated can be priceless.

Open Your Door to Solution-Focused School Counseling

As you begin to engage your administrator in the solution-focused approach, become more solution focused in everything you do at school. Since the solution-focused counselor thinks differently about school clients, meaning students, teachers, staff members, and parents, the method of helping others will be different. This counselor is not a problem solver; he's a solution investigator and collaborator. This often comes as a surprise when school staff members walk into the counselor's office asking for advice or a parent calls and demands a class be changed to accommodate her child, only to be asked, "How do you want things to be different?"

Kermit the Frog once said, "It's not easy being green." Neither is it easy for the counselor to stop giving advice and start putting responsibility back onto school clients. Yet when that happens, dynamic changes occur that make them self-sufficient. To start changing the approach and identifying goals and exceptions, the counselor has to set the stage first. There are several ways to do this. Here is one from the book *Narrative Counseling in Schools* by Winslade and Monk (2006). This note on the school counselor's door not only sets the stage, it also ignites curiosity:

Problem Busters
Services offered include:

- Lingering suspensions exterminated
- Bad reputations reversed
- Youth-to-adult conversions undertaken
- "Boredom" alleviated
- Trouble silenced
- Treaties with parents or teachers drawn up
- Miscellaneous problems neutralized, terminated, or otherwise gotten rid of

OUR MOTTO: The problem is the problem. The person is not the problem.

Up front, students, parents, and teachers know that this counselor is different. There is no blaming or complaining allowed in his office because it is not productive. Instead, people leave competent, with a direction for improvement.

Get Started in August

Once the administrator is on board, the solution-focused counselor should ask for time to meet with teachers at the first in-service in August, offering some tips for the classroom as school begins. Ideally the counselor should also let teachers know that he will be approaching issues differently this year on all levels. He should also mention that occasionally he will send e-mails requesting teachers to watch students differently, in addition to e-mails that (with student permission) describe student progress. Thereafter, a constant reminder that the approach is "going to last" can be given at faculty meetings, where additional solution-focused training can happen throughout the year.

To summarize setting the stage, these are the steps that have proven to be the most useful when solution-focused school counselors get ready to implement a solution-focused school program:

1. Take the School Strategy Survey, and study the results.
2. Talk to the administrator about the solution-focused approach and get buy-in.
3. Introduce the idea to teachers early in the year, sharing that it will help them with class management and teaching methods, in addition to helping their students become more responsible and more responsive.

The Field Guide to Counseling Toward Solutions

4. Keep the approach going through faculty training. Give monthly rewards for faculty members trying the approach. Consider a "solution-focused teacher of the month" award, where the teacher gives a brief synopsis to the staff of what he or she did that was solution focused. Then, provide a certificate for the teacher, and hang a copy in the faculty lounge.

5. Send e-mail commendations to teachers who try the approach.

6. Send weekly e-mails (see Chapter Six in this book) that inspire and allow teachers to brag on the progress that they see with the approach.

Pitfalls and Safeguards: Cooperate with the System First

The most important lesson I learned when working as a school counselor was to use the solution-focused approach with teachers as well as students. It took over a year to get started, but my perseverance and belief in the process paid off. The moral of this pitfall is to remember that everyone in the school is part of a large system. Everyone is your school client: teachers, students, parents, and school staff. As you begin trying new ideas such as those in this book, the system will become uncomfortable because change is not always welcomed. People in systems like to maintain their same roles because they know them. Asking them to change roles is anxiety provoking. Learn how your system reacts to change, and tread softly—but steadily.

This approach needs you to trust and believe in the model and stick with it even when the story and problem are more interesting to pursue. When I began working with the solution-focused model, I looked for exceptions too quickly, bypassing the need to clarify and specify what the school client wanted to achieve. I also forgot to explain my approach to teachers. I learned to inform school staff so that the system could collaborate with the student for success. I learned to wait, build the relationship with school clients, and get to know them and their abilities. Then I could inquire with lots of curiosity about what the school client wanted to achieve. That helped immensely. Then whenever I got stuck, I would ask myself:

"What do I need to do to cooperate with the school client more?"

"What does the school client want to accomplish, and is that different from what his teacher wants him to accomplish?"

"Am I letting my goal prevail instead of cooperating with the student's goal?"

These personal questions led me to ask the school client the same questions. On many occasions, I would say, "You know, we have been meeting for a few weeks, and I am curious about what you find helpful. Tell me what is helping." Their answers often surprised me and helped to get us back on track.

I learned that not everyone in my school would appreciate thinking in this new manner. As I developed the mentor program, a small group of teachers refused to work with me on the project, thinking that I was giving too much to the "offenders." Their thinking was steeped in pathology, consequences, and rewards, and they made comments like this one: "Why give a kid like him a chance? He didn't earn it." I soon learned to respect the fact that most teachers rarely, if ever, had learned problem-solving skills in their education classes. With that in mind, I resolved to see the teachers too as "without skills" at the moment to see the value of the program. Then when I saw them in the hallway, I would find something kind to say to them based on my honest observations of their classes, classroom decoration, or their dedication. When one of their students came to me for help, the student and I approached the teacher together with caution and respect. And when I asked the teacher to try something new, I always prefaced the request with, "I am as concerned about how this student affects your classroom as I am his success. What can I do for you as I work with him?" That brought cooperation from the teacher on many occasions.

Find a way to cooperate, and your program can get started.

Action Plan: Full Speed Ahead

This entire chapter is an action plan. As you begin contemplating how or when to begin, take a personal inventory about what works for you as well as your school staff:

- When am I at my best to sell this program to my administrator?
- What do I need to do for my school staff to let them know I am invested in this program?
- What would my school staff say that they need from me to begin implementing this program?
- How have I orchestrated the implementation of other programs?

No matter how small you begin, by thinking and viewing staff and school clients differently than in the past, you will start the ripple effect that will eventually reach everyone on your school campus. The time is now.

Chapter Two

Training Staff to Become Solution Focused

I said, "That was a very brave thing to do." He said, "Oh, it was just the training." I have a feeling that, in the end, probably that is the answer to a great many things.

—Elizabeth II

Schools are like families. Some teachers even refer to the school staff they work with as being "like family." Thompson, in his article, "Can Narrative Therapy Heal the School Family?" (2002), uses the word *family* because some schools are actually referred to as having a family feeling or as being dysfunctional like families by their staff. Thompson goes on to share his experience in the following passage on observing the school climate and the frustrating results that it can produce when the temperature is not right:

> It is impossible to spend any amount of time in small, independent schools without experiencing the emotional field that they generate. School faculties are optimistic together (in September), exhausted together (in February); they suffer together over illness, expulsions and parental criticism. In my experience, whole faculties share *transferential* reactions to school leaders, and are capable of having group depressions. Schools can have a professional atmosphere and a work-like climate, but if you spend any amount of time in them, you will experience them as emotional systems. Thinking in schools lags behind more traditional, individual psychological explanations. Though school leaders and teachers often sense or can see group effects, the explanations are usually individualistic and focus on a negative leader or leaders: The head of a school's story to a consultant is often something like: "We have a few older teachers in the upper school who are constantly complaining and it means we cannot institute any changes there because they always oppose us."

The faculty's story may be that: "The head of the lower school doesn't listen."

While these observations may in some sense be perfectly correct, they don't address the systemic issues or the school "story" which attempts to account for the systemic problems [p. 1].

The Family Reunion, Revisited

Sometimes families need reunions and activities to write new stories so that their members can begin to take on new roles. Davenport Community Schools in Iowa is a success story in that sense. When the district adopted a solution-focused approach, the administrators gathered principals, teachers, associate principals, school counselors, school psychologists, special education teachers, and aides together to learn the approach. Each person learned that he or she would have a new role—one of seeking strengths, resiliency, and abilities in their students and using those traits to construct solutions in the general education classroom. Although these new roles seemed appropriate and positive, they called for change. Change is not always easily accepted. It can be frightening to be expected to do something new without the right tools.

That's where the administrator comes in. As in families, the head of the household, that is, the principal, must share his or her support for the program with the staff. Many new techniques developed over the years in education have promised to change behaviors and increase motivation. Many of these ideas have been developed with good reason but were created by people outside schools. Because outsiders were presenting foreign ideas to school staff members, ownership didn't occur. Comments such as, "Well, it might work in Texas, but not Maryland," may filter through the school staff and undermine even the best attempts to share something new. But when it is the head of the school who supports the idea and wants to make it the school's project, different reactions occur that have a better chance of evolving into lasting change. To do this, the school family should become solution-focused educators as a team. Creating teamwork and an atmosphere of competency in schools is most successful when the school staff has a part in its development and implementation.

It is helpful to begin such a program by reviewing what has worked within the individual school. In the same way that the solution-focused approach seeks to elicit the competencies in students and parents, developing a school program among staff uses the same approach. Faculty members compose a rich source of resources, and the most effective solution-focused school counselor approaches the staff with this in mind.

Become the School with a Purpose

Like with the Cheshire Cat in *Alice in Wonderland,* solution-focused educators must know where they are going in order to get there. A possible way of beginning to know this is to ask the following questions during staff training and each faculty meeting whenever a new situation calls for a new approach:

"What is our purpose here as the faculty of this school?"

"When have we accomplished that in the past?"

"How did we do that?"

"Where are we currently, on a scale of 1 to 10, with 10 being the highest?"

For student issues: "Where would our students say we are?"

For parent issues: "Where would our parents say we are?"

"What do we need to do to slowly move up the scale?"

If these questions sound familiar, they are. These basic steps will surface throughout this field guide as ways to deal with practically any school issue. They are applicable to parents, teachers, administrators, coaches, nurses, and all other school staff members. Understanding the purpose or goal of a school gives direction in which to travel with students. The goal development process should include setting a goal agreeable to faculty members, helping teachers and administrators identify past successes, encouraging teamwork and collaboration, and putting into place a plan of action on a small scale. The most important component is to do what worked before. That ensures success.

Training Educators to Become Solution Focused

The next few pages include reproducible outlines for training staff members. Guidelines for making the training fun and personal are also given in the form of role plays and personal exercises. The most effective training begins in August and occurs in small increments each week or at each faculty meeting during the school year. The theme of "solution-focused approach" should be commonly understood and expected when it comes to working with students, parents, teachers, and teams. The training exercises after the initial meeting might begin this way to keep the theme going:

"What's going better in school?"

"Who's noticed colleagues doing things with students that seem to make a difference?"

These guiding questions allow teachers and administrators time to evaluate and trumpet their personal successes and note individual students in whom they see changes. Success is motivating to educators, and hearing peers describe their experiences encourages others to try the new ideas. Consider giving out a Solution-Focused Teacher of the Week award whenever possible. See a template at the end of this chapter.

The Solution-Focused School Program

Training Exercise 1: Problem Focused versus Solution Focused?

Begin talking to your staff about a new process called the *solution-focused school program*. Tell them it was originally a type of brief therapy developed by Steve de Shazer, from Milwaukee, in the early 1980s. As one of the originators of the solution-focused approach, de Shazer found at his agency that when clients got better, it wasn't the therapists whom they praised; it was the process. He grew interested in this phenomenon and learned that by talking to the solution-focused therapists, clients identified the "exceptions," or, times when problems did not occur as often, and then realized that they could solve their own problems. With this in mind, ask your school staff to tell you what they think the term *solution focused* means and how it might differ from *problem focused*. List their responses on a whiteboard, and compliment them on their answers. When you compliment, you begin the solution-focused process before their very eyes. That's more than just being positive; it's making them the experts, and when people feel like experts in their own lives, they are more likely to follow through with their own ideas. That promotes buy-in.

Tell the staff that the solution-focused process involves looking at times when problems happen slightly less often than usual. Tell them that the process is simple, but it requires a shift in thinking, from focusing on problems to identifying solutions. Then tell them that you are going to do a short exercise to introduce how different it is to be solution focused rather than problem focused. Say to them:

> Think of a student you are having some frustrations with. In pairs, turn to each other, and one person pretend to be the parent of that student and the other person be the teacher [or school counselor, depending on your audience]. Pretend that you have called a parent conference to discuss the problems. For the next five minutes, teachers [or school counselors] tell the parent what he or she needs to do to change the child. Tell the parent that maybe he or she needs to change as well. Those of you who are pretending to be the parent play your role as typically as possible. In other words, give the teachers a hard time!

You will get some laughter, perplexed looks, and even some scowls as you begin this exercise. Don't worry about the responses. You will soon see people frustrated as parents resolve not to listen to the problems told to them by the teachers. Don't offer any help; just move around the room, listen to the pairs discuss the exercise, and wait for approximately five minutes.

After five minutes, ask the group members to raise their hands if they were able to convince the parent that their child had a problem. There should be only a few hands raised, and maybe none at all. Ask, "Why do you think that it was so difficult to convince the parent that his or her child had a problem?" You may hear answers like these:

> "It was her child."
> "He was resistant."
> "She became defensive."
> "He wanted to blame the school."

Agree with them, and confirm that the process rarely works, yet in schools around the world, this is the very process that is used most often. Tell them that you now want them to try a new process. Pass out the Helpful Steps That Create a Solution-Focused Direction handout, but *only* to those "pretending to be teachers." Then say to the group:

> Let's try a different approach. Get into the same pairs, and talk about the same problems. The only difference is that those of you pretending to be teachers are now to use the handout that I have just given to you. The rest of you will get the handout later. Now begin following the handout. Try to get through each of the steps.

Helpful Steps That Create a Solution-Focused Direction

Using this sheet to jot down the answers will help you in learning the process.

Step 1: Talk about the concern.

"What can we talk about right now that would help you [your child] to be more successful? I care about what you think and what you need from me."

_____

_____

_____

_____

Step 2: Set the goal together.

"Tell me what it would look like on a small scale when things get better in the near future."

_____

_____

_____

_____

Step 3: Identify the exceptions together.

"Take me back to a time when a little of that happened, even in other situations. What was different then? What did you do differently? How did that make a difference for your child?"

_____

_____

_____

_____

_____

Helpful Steps That Create a Solution-Focused Direction (cont.)

Step 4: Ask the scaling question.

"On a scale of 1 of 10, with 1 meaning that things are not working and 10 meaning that things are perfect, where are things now in relation to our goal?"

_____

Step 5: Set a task for a short time period.

"On that same scale, where would you like to be by [establish the time: for example, one day, next week]?" _____

"What do you think needs to start happening so that can happen?" Go over the exception list as a reminder if necessary.

_____

_____

_____

_____

_____

_____

18

After about ten minutes, ask the group to talk about what was different using this approach rather than the first one. Write their answers down for everyone to see. Compliment them for their intuition. Ask them to tell you when they think this process could be used. Keep writing down as many answers as you are given. Keep asking, "What else?" and "When else?"

Let the staff know that your principal has endorsed the solution-focused process and that you will be implementing it with students, parents, and even them, the teachers, through your work as a school counselor. At this point, make sure everyone has a copy of the handout. Then encourage your principal to stand up and share with them his or her view of the process.

End by telling the faculty that in the near future, they may hear you use solution-focused terminology such as *exceptions* or *goals* with them whenever they send a student to you as a referral. You may also begin asking them to meet with you and the student to identify exceptions. In this way, not only the students get better, but classrooms run better too. Tell the teachers there may be times when they are asked to observe times when students do things better.

Training Exercise 2: Understanding the Solution-Focused Approach

Now that you have their interest, the rest of the faculty meeting can be informative as you go through the Solution-Focused Ideas to Remember handouts. There is one for you to read from and one to give the faculty. Feel free to reproduce them (and all others in this book). Talk about the short descriptions under each statement on your page, and invite faculty to comment on them. You may find that presenting just a few of the ideas during each faculty meeting and involving the staff in discussion about each idea is more time efficient if you are on a schedule during the faculty meeting. In addition, going slowly with these ideas is helpful in understanding them fully.

As the next few months unfold, add new solution-focused applications to existing programs or situations in your school, such as those described in this book for special education referrals, behavior interventions, crisis situations, parent conferences, teacher conferences, team meetings, and others. Do this by working with educators whom you feel influence other staff members in your school family. Those people are easy to identify. Try consulting with your principal and associate principals on who those people are, and work to win their support. By doing this, you have a better chance of creating buy-in and a better chance that the program will be accepted.

Solution-Focused Ideas to Remember: Faculty Copy

1. Using a nonpathological approach makes problems solvable.

2. It is not necessary to understand or promote insight to be helpful.

3. Always let the student (or parent) define the goal.

4. There is a ripple effect when one person changes.

5. Cooperate with the student's worldview, and you will lessen resistance.

6. If something works, don't change it. If it doesn't, do something different.

7. Go slowly, focusing on strengths and abilities in other situations.

8. Notice how and why behaviors happen, and always ask, "How did you do that?"

9. Realize that change is constant, and help students and parents to notice changes too.

10. Change the time and place, and you change the context for interactions.

Solution-Focused Ideas to Remember: Facilitator Copy

1. Using a nonpathological approach makes problems solvable.

Say: "As you saw in the first exercise, focusing on problems makes people resistant. Labeling our students puts them into categories that they can rarely escape from. What if, instead of labeling a student as ADD, we thought of him as energetic? What if, instead of labeling a student as defiant, we thought of her as expressing her opinion? How different would we react with these different labels?"

2. It is not necessary to understand or promote insight to be helpful.

Say: "You don't have time to uncover reasons that a student or parent acts or reacts as he or she does. And if you did find out why, that would not give you a direction to solutions. Instead, ask students about times when school went better and what they did to make that happen. That makes them responsible for change and builds them up. After you ask them what they did, ask what you can do, and see what happens. Even better, watch for times when school goes better for the most challenging students. Talk to your colleagues who have the same student, and find out how they deal with the student effectively and learn what the student responds to, even if slightly."

3. Always let the student (or parent) define the goal.

Say: "Sometimes we get stuck as educators when we try to make our goal the student's goal. That rarely works. As you saw in the second exercise, when you asked the parent what he thought would be a sign that things were better, the goal was different. Maybe it was, 'I won't get a phone call from the school.' Although your goal is to see the student behave better, both goals work to accomplish the same result. The same result can happen with students by saying: 'Mo, when I look through your grades, I see that you turned in five out of eight assignments. I am curious how you turned in those five. What do you think you could do to turn in six out of eight next week?'"

4. There is a ripple effect when one person changes.

Say: "Here's an interesting experiment. Just for the next day, pick out a student who challenges you, but before this happens, do something different from the way you usually interact, such as ask about the student's backpack and all of the stickers on it. Talk to the student before class and say that you appreciate her getting to class almost on time. Mention to her after class that you liked her ability to pay attention a little more that day. This is not just being positive; it is pointing out the exceptions. Notice what happens when you do things differently. Another idea is to tell a challenging student on Tuesday that you would like to write a note to his parent on Friday about his good behavior that week. Tell him that you will be watching for things to say in the letter. [For elementary students,

Solution-Focused Ideas to Remember: Facilitator Copy (cont.)

this should be for one or two days; for middle school, two to three days; and for high school, three to four days]." Then ask the group: "Why do you think we would try this for only a few days?" The answer you hope to get will be words to this effect: "It's easier to succeed in a shorter time."

5. Cooperate with the student's worldview, and you will lessen resistance.

Say: "How many of you who pretended to be parents in the first exercise felt a little resistant when you were told that your child had a problem? The same thing happens with our students. Instead of forcing a solution that is ours, look for a solution that cooperates with where the student is. For example, if Hideki can't sit still, let him stand to do his work, and tell him to do so, he has to do it quietly. If Gina has to talk constantly, tell her that you will give her five minutes to talk all she wants to with her friend Priya when she completes her assignment. If a student needs your constant attention, try to give that attention to him whenever you can, and get him to help you with classroom chores. Above all, if the student's goal is simply to pass your class, say that is a great goal and that you want to hear his strategy for doing that. Cooperating with your students will make your life a lot stressful."

This idea is sometimes controversial and may raise a few eyebrows. So be ready for questions such as, "What if what they need from us is not possible, such as changing an assignment or a grade?" Advise them to listen nevertheless because that listening is vital to the process. Then tell them to ask the student, "How will it help you if I change the assignment?" Chances are the student will tell the teacher something like, "I will be able to do it better." Ask again: "How will that help you?" The student may say, "I can pass. I need to pass.""Then together, talk about other ways that you can help the student pass. Offer additional assignments for extra credit, or ask the student what else you can do to help him pass. Talk about how he has passed other challenging classes before, and tell him you are interested in being part of the team that gets him to pass."

6. If something works, don't change it. If it doesn't, do something different.

Say: "We have heard the old adage, 'Insanity is the art of doing the same thing that doesn't work, over and over again.' I think that in schools, sometimes we forget to try new ideas. The next time that you run into resistance from a student, do something different. A school teacher in California had a clipboard that she had fastened a huge bright red paper clip to. Whenever a student she had tried to get back on task did not comply, she gave the clipboard to the student and told her to go to the office. The office staff had been prepared to watch for the bright red paper clip, and whenever a student arrived with it, they greeted the student and give him or her a short chore to do in the office. When the student finished, the staff was to wildly compliment the student and send her back to

Solution-Focused Ideas to Remember: Facilitator Copy (cont.)

class. The teacher said that just doing something different made all the difference. When the student returned, she was thanked and later told that it was known in the office what a good worker she was. When you change relationships with students, you change their behavior."

7. Go slowly, focusing on strengths and abilities in other situations.

Say: "In every classroom there are students who do things outside class that are exceptional. Maybe there is a Boy Scout who gets badges because he completes his assignments. Ask how he can use those skills with his work that day. There are adolescents who have jobs at night and keep those jobs because they are prompt to them. Ask how they get there on time when they are tardy to your class. There are even students who seem to have poor motivation everywhere but the soccer field, where they are stars. Ask them what makes the difference there that keeps them so well disciplined and motivated. Although you can't be a scout leader, boss, or coach, in some ways you can borrow what those adults do with the students. You can even use the same strategies with parents who feel stuck on how to work with their own children. Talk about the skills they have at work and how they can adapt those skills to home life."

8. Notice how and why behaviors happen, and always ask, "How did you do that?"

Say: "Exceptions are everywhere. Think of all that you have done this week that didn't go well. Now think of the times when life went smoother. Can you recall them? It's more difficult because those times don't stand out like the difficult periods. But within those times are our solutions. This week, notice times when your most troubling students are slightly better. Notice when you feel less stressed, and notice when the lesson plan goes really well. Jot down those times, and repeat those successes again and again."

9. Realize that change is constant, and help students and parents notice changes too.

Say: "I'm asking you to notice times when students do better, so why not ask students to do the same? Maybe they talk about another teacher they don't get along with, yet they get along with everyone else. Ask them what they might do to help themselves get along with the others that they sometimes forget to do with the teacher of concern. The same tactic can be helpful to students who talk about home problems: their parents yell or stay on their backs perhaps. By talking about times when their parents aren't on their backs, students might be able to identify what they have done differently to help that to happen.

Solution-Focused Ideas to Remember: Facilitator Copy (cont.)

"With parents, asking to do the same with their children may give them an opportunity to look for times when their children do what they need them to do. If they can't answer, you can ask: 'What would they say you have done differently before?' This gives them a new way to think about things."

10. Change the time and place, and you change the context for interactions.

Say: "Are there certain times when you don't mind talking about things? Are there certain days that you don't mind dealing with things? The same goes for students. If telling a student to settle down in class doesn't work, try taking the student into the hallway and being straight with him or her by saying: "Mary, I'm stuck. I have tried to let you know what I need you to do, but it hasn't worked. I am interested in our working together so that your talking doesn't keep you from completing your work. What can we do to finish out this class in a good way, just for today?" Mary will see your frustration and your true desire to reach her. Many students rarely see this side of their teacher, and it can have different results. Change the time, the place, or anything else, and, according to the laws of physics, things will react differently."

Training Exercise 3: Creating Possibilities Through Language

Explain that a way to reach students is by redescribing the presented problem of a student into "solution-talk":

1. On a whiteboard, write these categories, each as a column heading: "Problem Talk," "Strategies," "Solution Talk," and "New Strategies." Ask the staff for descriptions of students who are challenging them now. List them under "Problem Talk."

2. Ask the staff to tell you what their current strategies are to deal with those challenges. Write their answers under "Strategies." Ask the staff members to tell you whether each strategy works in the long term. Mark a line through those strategies that they say do not work.

3. Ask the staff to change the descriptions under "Problem Talk" to more benign behaviors. For example, "ADHD" becomes "energetic." Write their answers under "Solution Talk."

4. Erase the descriptions under "Problem Talk."

5. Ask for strategies for dealing with the new descriptions, and write them down under "New Strategies."

6. Ask the staff what they learned from this exercise. Mention that you are not sugar-coating student actions; you are instead redescribing them so that they as a school staff can discover new ways of dealing with the same students.

7. Assign the staff the task of identifying one student over the next week who might have had a Problem Talk description. Ask the staff to come up with a Solution Talk description and new strategies. Ask the staff to e-mail you their completed assignment before the next faculty meeting.

Training Exercise 4: Scale Problems Down to Size

Ask for two volunteers. One staff member is to be Sarah, and another staff member is to portray Sarah's mom.

Tell the staff that you are doing a role play to help them understand how using the scaling question can facilitate a productive conversation. Let them know that each of them could do what the school counselor is doing in the conversation. After the role play, ask the staff to describe what they think made the conversation helpful.

SCHOOL COUNSELOR: Mom, you say that you are having a hard time trusting your daughter Sarah since she has failed three classes and skipped school three times this term. Is that correct?

MOM: Yes, it's hard to trust her at all. (scowling at Sarah) I would like to trust her again, but it will take a long time.

SCHOOL COUNSELOR: Sarah, where would you say you are right now on a scale of 1 to 10, where 1 means you are not trusted at all by Mom and 10 means you are totally trusted?

SARAH: About a 2.

MOM: That's even lower than I would have said!

SCHOOL COUNSELOR: Sarah, where would you like to be by the time I meet with you again?

SARAH: At least a 5, but I don't know if that will make a difference to her.

SCHOOL COUNSELOR: Mom, would that make a difference?

MOM: Anything will make a difference.

SCHOOL COUNSELOR: Sarah, you say you are at a 2 now and want to move up to a 5 by next week. What would you suggest you do to move up three places?

SARAH: Probably come home and do homework so she sees me trying at least. Not skipping school would probably help.

SCHOOL COUNSELOR: Mom, would that make a difference?

MOM: Maybe.

SARAH: See, she's so negative!

SCHOOL COUNSELOR: I guess that happens sometimes when the trust level goes down. What I'm interested in, though, are your ideas and the fact that Mom has been able to trust you before. Have ideas like this helped to gain your mom's trust before?

SARAH: Yeah, sort of. I think she trusted me last year when I studied at home and didn't skip. She spent time with me too.

SCHOOL COUNSELOR: Is this true?

MOM: Yes. I remember last year was a better year.

SCHOOL COUNSELOR: Looking back, where would you have placed Sarah on the same scale we've been talking about last year?

MOM: Probably an 8.

SCHOOL COUNSELOR: That's great! What did she do then to be that high on your trust level?

MOM: She studied, and her grades were good. She came home when I asked her, and her friends came over so I got to meet them instead of wondering who they are.

SCHOOL COUNSELOR: So, Sarah, you already know how to do this.

SARAH: I guess.

SCHOOL COUNSELOR: Go for it. Sounds like a 5 is a very reasonable idea for this week. I want you to keep thinking, too, where you want to end up on that scale. Okay?

SARAH: Okay.

SCHOOL COUNSELOR: Mom, I'd like you to pay particular attention this week to specific things that Sarah does to make your trust level with her rise. Okay?

MOM: Okay.

Training Exercise 5: The Problem Is the Problem

Thinking about problems as external frees people from feeling as if *they* are the problem.

For this exercise, ask for one volunteer to read aloud the teacher's part in the next dialogue while you read the counselor's part. Afterward, ask the staff how the questions assist the teacher in seeing the problem of "depression" (her description) differently. Focus on how much more responsible the teacher is in doing something about the depression when she sees it as external. The same process can work for students. Suggest how using words such as *anger, fighting habit, talking habit,* and *forgetfulness* and talking about them as external with students help everyone to band together to fight the problem.

COUNSELOR: How has this *depression* interfered with your ability to teach effectively?

TEACHER: It keeps me from enjoying my students, being creative in the holiday activities I used to love doing, and looking forward to the next day.

COUNSELOR: How have you let the depression take over sometimes and intrude in your life, keeping you from these things that you just described to me?

TEACHER: Well, I go home and I just sit, or I go to school and think about how bad things are since Bob left me, or I think that things will never get better.

COUNSELOR: How many hours a day would you say you let the depression bother you?

TEACHER: It's worse in the morning for about an hour and then at night, for about three hours.

COUNSELOR: So, four hours a day?

TEACHER: Yes.

COUNSELOR: What about the other waking hours of the day? How many would that leave?

TEACHER: About eight, I guess.

COUNSELOR: How do you keep the depression from bothering you during those hours?

TEACHER: I'm here at school or doing things for my kids at home.

COUNSELOR: How do you keep the depression from bothering you so that you are able to do things here at school or for your children? That's incredible.

TEACHER: I have to. I have to do certain things to survive.

COUNSELOR: That's great! With all this going on, you still think ahead of what you need to do, about surviving because you know you have to.

TEACHER: Yes, the kids depend on me.

COUNSELOR: What does that do for you?

TEACHER: Makes me feel important, needed, wanted.

COUNSELOR: Who else does that?

TEACHER: I guess the teachers here, friends, my family.

COUNSELOR: So you have quite a support system who needs you, wants you around, sees you as important?

TEACHER: I never thought of it that way, but yes, I do.

Training Exercise 6: Writing Solutions

Make copies of Notes 1 and 2, and hand them to your staff members, or incorporate them into a PowerPoint presentation. The situation is about a twelve-year-old boy who cannot concentrate in class. Ask them how different Note 1 is from Note 2 and discuss.

Note 1

To: Parents of Joey Smith

I am writing you and including the grades that your son is currently making in class. He is in jeopardy of failing the semester if his grades do not improve.

Please speak with Joey about this matter. His tendency to be distracted is causing much of the problem. If I can do anything to help, let me know.

Thank you,

Ms. Concerned

Note 2

Dear Joey,

I wanted to write you this note to tell you how impressed I am that you have been in control of the "energy" for the past day. Wow. It's nice to see you in charge for a change instead of "energy." I noticed that your classmates treated you much differently. Did you? Let's talk soon about how you've done this. I am very impressed with you!

Ms. Observant

Pitfalls and Safeguards: Families Need Tender Loving Care

Families resist change because it means that their roles change. As you begin the process of training staff, make sure that your school family realizes that you are there to help them with the process that promises to help their class management as well as their students. This will be a comfort to them and will not put the burden of "another new project" on them alone. Solidify this comfort by writing anonymous notes occasionally, complimenting them on their progress. When one school counselor did that in Irving, Texas, she found that she had dramatically fewer referrals from teachers who had seemed to refer more than their share of students in the past. As the year ended, the same counselor received thank-you notes from those teachers.

The beauty of the solution-focused model is in the eyes of the beholder—in this case, in the eyes of your school family. As you help them in teams and with individual parents and students, you may see their eyes brighten as change occurs. This is what sells the model to educators. Be patient and curious. Ask teachers who refer students to you how they coped as long as they did with the challenging student. Mention to the teachers that you are interested in how they have worked with other challenging students. For teachers who continue to be problem focused, compliment them on their ability to see problems so clearly. Then, drawing on their keen observation skills, ask them to watch for something different—a time when the problem doesn't appear as often, just for a day.

And just maybe, there will be a family reunion at the end of the school year where problems aren't discussed at all, only solutions. You can always dream.

Action Plan: Notice the Family Favorites

For Elementary Schools

Once after I gave a workshop to a staff at an elementary school, the principal came over to me and said she realized that there were certain teachers in her school who never referred students to her or to the counselors. She said they were like "miracle workers" in her school. We both mused at the idea, and I mentioned to her that I thought she might use that concept with referrals. I suggested that she might gather together an initial "miracle worker" team at the beginning of the school year, composed of those nonreferring teachers, and train them to work with students and teachers in the solution-focused approach.

From that concept, the idea grew in her school to be a valuable resource. The school counselor facilitated the team process initially and trained the initial miracle workers. Thereafter, she was able to step away and let the team function on its own. The principal started with the true miracle workers and throughout the school year asked every teacher on the staff to serve on the team at least once during the year. Each time the team changed, one seasoned member remained for a week to teach the ropes to the new miracle workers. The referrals to the school counselor plummeted, and the staff became more competent.

If you are an elementary school counselor, begin implementing the school program by sharing this chapter with your principal and explaining your role in the transition from a problem-focused approach to a solution-focused approach. As you develop the miracle workers in your school, let the staff know that whenever they have a difficulty with a student, they can refer to the miracle workers team, and the team members will begin the process. Tell the teachers that this will require them to identify exceptions to complete the referral. The teachers may find that as they inquire about exceptions, the referral is not necessary.

Choose a place where the miracle workers' referrals can be easily found, such as the teacher's lounge or near teacher mailboxes. Glance over the Miracle Worker Referral Form, and make copies for your school. You may choose to add your school logo to the form to customize it.

Spend time training the miracle workers to follow the steps on the Miracle Workers Conversation Script that follows the referral form. Reproduce the script, and go over the questions, explaining their purpose. You may find that the teachers grasp the ideas rather quickly (because they do not have counseling theories to battle) and find them a welcome reprieve from a problem-solving approach. As you can imagine, their classrooms will benefit from their new-found knowledge as well. Keep watching for changes that they make as a result of being on the miracle worker team, and compliment them as often as possible. Since this program will undoubtedly be under your supervision as the school counselor, you will need to sit in on their meetings to help them stay on track and focus on solutions initially. However, you may find that the miracle workers will use the time much more efficiently than in the past in problem-focused meetings. This will help you deal with many referrals quickly and sort through referrals that you need to give special attention to. Best of all, your staff will become competent at handling many situations comfortably.

For Secondary Schools

Talk to your alternative school principal (or campus principal if your district does not have an alternative school), and invite her to participate in a mentor program that you coordinate. Promote your program by mentioning that you are trying to decrease the number of students who return to alternative school and increase student motivation and success.

Take the following steps to ensure that your program gets buy-in.

1. Give to each student entering the alternative school (or your home campus) The Mentor Program Student Survey. (A reproducible copy is at the end of the chapter.) It provides the staff at both the alternative school and the home campus a snapshot of the student's worldview. The survey is short, and you need to read probably only twenty to thirty at the beginning of the semester to get a random sample of what students are thinking, feeling, and needing. By giving this survey to students when they enroll in the alternative school, you can get parental permission at that time. If you do not have an alternative program, consider getting parental approval nevertheless.

2. Get buy-in from the staff. After you receive at least twenty to thirty surveys, tally the answers, and ask for a few minutes at your next faculty meeting to share the results with staff at your home campus. Begin by sharing your desire to help teachers conduct their classrooms in a manageable fashion. Discuss the difficulties for both teachers and students when students return from the alternative campus. Talk about the survey, which you can refer to as "an experiment," as a means to understand where the students are emotionally and behaviorally. Then read the results slowly. Afterward ask the staff what the students are saying that they need from everyone. Describe the mentor plan you are establishing to achieve what the students need. Then pass out three- by five-inch note cards to the staff, asking them to fill in their name and room number on the card if they would like to be a mentor. Mention that a mentor will be a staff member who simply communicates with a student while he or she is in the alternative school (or on campus) and then meets as often as they like when the student returns. As the year progresses, there will be social functions where mentors and mentored students can gather. Thank the teachers for their participation.

3. Match the student with a staff member. Arrange with the principal or secretary at the alternative school to inform you when a student is sent to the alternative school and request that The Mentor Program Student Information Sheet be sent to you. This program is set up so that there can be continuous communication between alternative and home campuses. By creating this relationship between the two schools, students are not left out of the loop, and when they return to the home campus, the chances that they will stay there, with a mentor's help, increase. Match up the mentored student with a mentor. Then send a letter to the student at the alternative school about the mentor program and identify the mentor for the student and include an envelope addressed to the mentor for the student's note. (See The Mentor Program reproducible at the end of the chapter.) Then send a copy of the Student Information Sheet to the mentor. It may help to provide an envelope for the mentor to use for the initial correspondence. Use your school intercampus mail system if allowable.

4. Get information on what has worked with the student. When the mentored student is ready to return to the home campus, request that the Teacher Observation Sheet: Alternative School Success be completed by each of the alternative school teachers and have it faxed or sent to you. (The reproducible is at the end of the chapter.) Copy the sheet, and give it to each classroom teacher.

5. Reintroduce the student at the home campus. When the mentored student returns, greet her and welcome her back to campus. Show the Teacher Observation Sheet to the student and mention that it has been distributed to all of her teachers. Ask the student to tell you how she wants things to go for her during the first week. This will give you information to share with teachers through e-mail, with the student's permission.

Consider notifying the Parent-Teacher Association or other school volunteer organizations about the mentor program and encourage them to donate treats for holidays that you can place in mentors' mailboxes. Inquire at local restaurants about a discount for pizza or fast food that you can provide twice each semester at a social gathering for mentors and mentored students. T-shirts can be designed by students and a designated day of the week can be Mentor Day. (Contact showyourlogo.com for great T-shirt rates or your local T-shirt store for discounts.)

Adapt the forms that follow to your own needs, and add your school logo to them. Then you will be off and running toward solutions.

Miracle Workers Referral Form

Student Name: _____

Date: _____

Referring Teacher: _____

What is happening in the classroom to cause your concern?

_____

_____

On a scale of 1 to 10, with 1 being the worst and 10 being completely successful, where is the student currently in regard to the concern? _____

What will the student be doing in the classroom over the next few weeks so that the scaling score increases?

_____

_____

What have you tried to solve this concern?

_____

_____

Before submitting this form, please ask your colleagues about times when this concern occurs less often in their classrooms. Summarize their responses:

_____

_____

Please indicate a good day and time for us to meet with you and your student for approximately fifteen minutes: _____

Thank you,

The Miracle Workers

Miracle Workers Conversation Script

Student Name: _____

Date: _____

Referring Teacher: _____

To the team: Say the items that are in italics, just as they are written.

To the teacher and student: *We are happy to work with you today. Our job is to help you identify what you both want in the classroom and to help you discover ways to begin making that happen. Our names are* [say your names].

To the teacher: *Please introduce us to your student and tell us some things about him or her that will inform us about his or her abilities in or out of school.* Write down the teacher's answers below:

_____

_____

_____

1. Concern

To both teacher and student: *First, tell us what has gone slightly better since you turned in the referral form?* If there has been some progress, inquire about what the teacher or student did differently. If nothing has changed, proceed to the next question.

_____

_____

_____

2. Goal

To the teacher: *What will the student be doing in the classroom over the next week that will tell you things are better?* Write down the answers below:

_____

_____

_____

Miracle Workers Conversation Script (cont.)

To the student: *What will be happening for you when things get better?* Help the student to be specific, as if a video camera filmed the success. Write down the answers below:

_____

_____

_____

To the student: *What will your teacher be doing to help make this happen, on a small scale?* Write down the answers below:

_____

_____

_____

To the student: *What will you be doing to help make this happen, on a small scale?* Write down the answers below:

_____

_____

_____

3. Exceptions

To both teacher and student: *When is this happening slightly already—in your classroom, other classrooms, and situations at school or even outside school?* Consider asking about traits of the student in other situations, such as a job, scouts, or being a Big Brother/Big Sister, that could be helpful in the current concern. Write down the answers below:

_____

_____

_____

4. Strategy development

To both teacher and student: *Based on what you have both said today, we would like to read back what you have told us* [read the exceptions in item 3] *and together with you come up with a plan for* [a day, for a child; a week, for an adolescent].

Miracle Workers Conversation Script (cont.)

To the student: *From what I have just read, what would you like to try that has already worked, just for the next* [specified time]*?*

_____

_____

_____

To the teacher: *From what I have just read, what would you like to try that has already worked, just for the next* [specified time]*?*

_____

_____

_____

5. Scale

To teacher and student: *On a scale of 1 to 10, with a 10 being that things are just like you want them to be and a 1 meaning that things are not working, where were you when you came in today? Where would you like to be in* [specified time]*?*

_____

_____

_____

To both teacher and student: *To end our conversation, we are interested in what was helpful for you today.*

_____

_____

_____

To teacher: *Please notify our team in a week to tell us what is going better.*

The Mentor Program Student Survey

Please answer the following questions as honestly as possible. Do not put your name on this paper because it is confidential. That means that no one here at school will know that these are your answers. This survey is designed to help you help your school improve its services to you.

Use the numbers below to answer the questions. Circle the number that fits your answer:

1 = never,   2 = sometimes,   3 = always

1.	When I am at school, I feel good about myself.	1	2	3
2.	My teachers help me to be the best that I can be.	1	2	3
3.	When I am upset, I talk to an adult.	1	2	3
4.	I feel scared at school.	1	2	3
5.	I know what it is like to feel depressed.	1	2	3
6.	I feel safe at my home.	1	2	3
7.	I get into fights when I need to solve a problem.	1	2	3
8.	My family is supportive of me.	1	2	3
9.	When I do something wrong, I am punished fairly.	1	2	3
10.	I think my teachers care about me.	1	2	3

The Mentor Program

Dear _____ ,

Congratulations, you have a mentor!

Your mentor is _____

Who is a _____

at your school. While you are in the alternative school, you will receive letters from your mentor, who wants to support you in your efforts to get you back on track at school.

When you receive a letter from your mentor, please respond by using the enclosed envelope. Give the envelope to your teacher at the alternative school and ask that it be mailed to your home campus.

I look forward to meeting you very soon.

_____
School Counselor

The Mentor Program Student Information Sheet

Dear Student,

While you are at the alternative campus, you will have a mentor from the home campus who will write to you occasionally. The information that you share will help the mentor get to know you. It will only be given to the mentor and it will be confidential.

Your Name: _____   Grade: _____

Home Campus: _____

Describe your interests, hobbies, and what you like to do outside school.

_____

_____

_____

_____

_____

What do you hope to accomplish while you are at the alternative campus?

_____

_____

_____

What do you need from your home campus teachers when you return that would be helpful to you?

_____

_____

_____

Thanks for your time.

_____

School Counselor

Teacher Observation Sheet:
Alternative School Success

Dear Teacher,

Your student, _____, will return to his or her home campus very soon. Your observations of what has been helpful to the student while in your class will be very important to the home campus teachers. Below, please write down what you have noticed as **helpful** teaching strategies, as well as classroom management strategies that seemed to work with this student.

Teaching Methods That Work

1. _____

2. _____

3. _____

4. _____

5. _____

Description of behavior. Please list positive traits that you observed about this student in your classroom:

_____

_____

_____

_____

_____

_____   _____
Your Signature   Subject/Classroom

Solution-Focused Teacher of the Week!

THIS CERTIFIES THAT

_____

has portrayed the traits of a solution-focused teacher
by the following solution-focused traits:

_____

_____

_____

The Staff at _____ School

sees this teacher as a model for us all!

_____

Principal

Chapter Three

Working Together with Teams, Teachers, and Parents

*Leadership is based on inspiration, not Domination,
on cooperation, not intimidation.*

—William Arthur Wood

Chris Hooker is a wraparound facilitator of a program for at-risk youth. A wraparound facilitator leads a team that may be composed of counselors, occupational therapists, social workers, and other mental health practitioners and with the team plans interventions to help the youth succeed. Chris's job involves such a team which has taken him into the homes of many adolescents where he and a team of behavior interventionists work with the family and the acting-out adolescent to increase school and home success. Before he learned the solution-focused process, Chris told me that he would become frustrated with the process, which tended to focus on problems. This often led to a long process of struggling with the adolescent in an effort to get him or her to admit to having problems and submit to solutions. Chris, a diligent worker who believes that competency, not deficits, is the key to solutions, wanted to do something different. The following story that he has written for this chapter is one where he did just that.

Case Study: A Focus on Competence, by Chris Hooker

Mike is a fourteen-year-old African American who has been in and out of several alternative schools. He lives with his grandparents and does not have contact with either of his biological parents. Mike also has been on probation at different times for getting into fights with other students and being verbally aggressive with teachers. He has been participating in the Wraparound Program with his grandparents. I had set up several meetings at both the school and at home. The following wraparound meeting took place at Mike's newest alternative school with his grandmother, teacher, two behavior interventionists, and school administrator. Mike was not present at the meeting because he did not want to participate.

I began by explaining to those present that the main focus of the wraparound program is to look at the strengths of the family and child and try to build on these strengths. I pointed out that Mike loves sports, especially football and basketball. I also mentioned that Mike can be very funny and that he has a great smile. I then asked the behavior interventionists about some of the things that were going on at school. They listed several problems that mostly focused on being disruptive in class and often having anger outbursts. When I heard the problem-focused descriptions, I was concerned that the problems might take control of the meeting and set a negative atmosphere. Therefore, I attempted to redirect the meeting with an exception-finding question to find out times when Mike was not being as disruptive at school. The behavior interventionists were initially surprised by this question and did not have an answer. Gradually, however, the following exceptions emerged:

- The program coordinator stated that Mike did get upset with a student once and made the choice to remain on campus when he wanted to leave.
- Another behavior interventionist said that Mike does better when he has staff members close by during class time.
- The team concluded that Mike had a great personality and was enjoyable to be around in one-on-one situations.

The program coordinator also noted that unfortunately Mike could not play on the school basketball team because registration had already passed. Pleased with the turnaround in the conversation toward strengths, I suggested that we meet again in two weeks with Mike present.

Two weeks later, another meeting was held with Mike and his grandmother present. The program coordinator, behavior interventionists, and two additional teachers attended the meeting. Since the previous meeting, the school had allowed Mike to play on the school basketball team in an effort to be flexible, to show that they recognized his strengths, and to give him a chance. A behavior interventionist took Mike to a Golden Glove boxing competition, and the program coordinator reported improved behavior at school. The team meeting had a different tone, and all of the staff members listed a litany of positives related to Mike and his interaction with the teachers. One teacher stated that she was still having difficulty with Mike in the classroom, but that complaint did not turn out to be the main theme of the meeting.

Mike did not talk much during the meeting, but he smiled several times and appeared to be taking in the positive feedback from the staff. One of his teachers volunteered to work with him for twenty minutes after school each day to bring up his grades. The teacher also said that he wanted to keep working with Mike after he returned to regular school to ensure that he continued to be successful. The grandmother also reported improved behavior at home and better communication with Mike. The team informed Mike that they would continue to explore his strengths and focus on the progress he was making at home and school.

Help Them Grow

It is common for school counselors to be a member of a team such as the one that Chris described, where the focus is on working through the problems and issues of a student. Too often, however, the focus becomes that of listing the deficits of a student or parent, and that exercise leads nowhere. These negative descriptions are often given in good faith: those who refer students feel that the school counselor and the team must truly understand how bad things are in order to help the student or parent. Inevitably questions and statements such as the following intrude on the process and keep the team from being as helpful as they can:

"He's just like his older brother, and *he's* in jail."

"She did fine during the beginning of the year, until she joined the peewee cheerleading squad, and now she's obsessed with being popular."

"With parents like that, no wonder she has this problem."

"I can do my part, but until his parents get him medication, there's little I can do."

"If I bend the rules for him, I will have to bend them for everyone else, and that's not fair to those who already work hard."

"A child his age shouldn't be having tantrums. There must be something wrong."

"There is no reason for his failure. He's bright, but he just won't turn work in, and until he does, there's little I can do."

These statements can poison any well-intentioned team process and stifle its creativity because the focus is on the problem, not the solution. Most team members mean well. They want to help students, but they have only a few interventions in their bag of tricks, and when those techniques don't work, the team begins to think that the problem is outside their expertise. When Chris Hooker brought up a new, exception-finding question to inquire about times when Mike behaved better, the behavior interventionists were speechless at first. They had been so focused on identifying problem times that they had not noticed when the negative behaviors were happening less often; that is they were the exceptions.

Yet it is within the exceptions that people can begin to discover answers. And by presenting such a novel idea to a team, Chris found that other reactions occurred; for example, the coach became flexible and gave Mike a chance to play basketball. By introducing such ideas to teams, the solution-focused school counselor not only changes the process and the possibilities for the student, but changes the thinking of the teachers. This can lead to a ripple effect. As teachers begin to watch for exceptions, they realize that the student might have strengths that they had not noticed before. This leads to a change of approach by the teacher, and typically the student responds differently as well.

A New Dialogue to Solutions

The following description of a team meeting about a student named Jill shows how to interrupt the problem-focused approach and introduce the solution-focused approach. If you choose to have the student in the meeting, include the student in each question. And if you suspect that a team is particularly frustrated with a student, talk to the team first, without the student present, to set the mood for solutions; then invite the student in.

At the end of this section is the Team Summary of Exceptions worksheet that the team will use in the meeting. The school counselor's introduction that follows is written to correspond to that worksheet, and the numbers used here correspond to those on the worksheet as well.

1. *Presenting the issue of concern:* "Everyone here certainly has Jill's best interest at heart. You have definitely described a student with issues that I will address when I meet with her."

2. *How the team will know when the problem is solved:* "One thing that I would like you to think about is how you will know when these issues are resolved. For example, imagine a day when Jill comes to your classroom and the problems we are discussing are absent. What will she be doing differently?"

3. *Identifying exceptions:* "Now, please look at your grade books, and find the times and situations where the problems aren't as prevalent. Look at homework assignments that Jill turned in, days when her behavior was almost appropriate, times when she did not disrupt the class, or times when she was slightly more polite than usual. As you tell me about those times, I am going to write down what you find."

4. *Tasks for meeting team goals:* "Based on what you have each just told me, what would you suggest doing just for the next week, until our next meeting, to help Jill?"

5. *Contacting the student:* "I'd like to share with Jill that you are going to be trying some new ways of working with her. I won't tell her what you are doing, but I will ask her to watch closely."

As you gather this information, if Jill is not present, take the exceptions to your next session with Jill and, with the team's permission, talk to her about what the team discovered. Jill will probably be surprised, and this will ultimately work systemically since she will begin seeing her teachers as more than just punitive and disappointed in her. Ideally, the next step might be to meet again with the team and Jill to discuss what Jill thinks she could do more of to get a longer list of exceptions. The face-to-face interaction as this occurs is invaluable to changing not only Jill's behavior, but the attitudes of her teachers, who will see her differently as well. And here's a hint on how to end the meeting: ask Jill what it is like for her to hear what the teachers are trying to do for her. As she replies, her teachers may hear a different side of Jill. This is a powerful moment that can change teacher-student relationships in a positive way. Whenever I have used this approach with teams in middle school and high school with the student present, I rarely had to follow up with the student because change happened quickly thereafter. The premise is simple: change the teacher-student relationship, and you change behavior.

Team Summary of Exceptions

Date: _____

Student: _____ Team: _____

1. Presenting issue of concern to the team:

_____

_____

_____

2. How the team will know when the problem is solved:

_____

_____

_____

3. Exceptions: Times when the issue is less of a problem according to team members:

_____

_____

_____

_____

4. Tasks for meeting team goals, based on exceptions:

_____

_____

_____

_____

5. Contact the student: Share that the team will try new strategies.

Just Take Him Away!

If a student is particularly troublesome to a few teachers on the team, it may be difficult to steer them toward a solution-focused process. The teachers may need to vent their feelings and frustrations before you begin the process. Listen to them, and then listen some more. They need to be heard; after all, they are your school clients too. Then empathize with them, and begin to explore the new approach. Gentle coaxing into a better way of processing will pay off in the future. This is called "cooperating with where your school client is." Cooperation cannot happen without effective goal setting. The goal in this case will end up being your goal rather than the team goal, and you will miss an opportunity to hear what the team is truly trying to accomplish.

For example, if you hear that the team would like the student removed because he is such a disruption, ask: "So what would that do for your classes if he was moved to alternative school?" and then: "And how would that make a difference?" You may then hear, "I can get through the curriculum and give the students who really need the attention what they need from me." By talking to teachers on a team in this manner, the counselor appears more empathetic, more patient with their frustration, and more cooperative. From this point, begin talking to the teachers about how they could begin to "teach again." What would a plan B look like if student X is not removed from class? Brainstorm with them what they could do for each other or with each other or what you could do.

I once worked with a student who was labeled in this manner by his algebra teacher and gave him a permanent pass for days when his teacher and he could not get along. After the first fifteen minutes of instruction, he could get his work and come to my office, where he would complete it. Some of my colleagues were afraid that he would abuse the privilege, but he didn't. I gave him a few permanent passes and apparently simply knowing he had this option, and the control that went with it, was enough because he did not always use the pass.

Case Study: Recognizing the Parents as Experts on Their Child, by Nicole Lucas Shannon

Nicole Lucas Shannon received her master's degree from Texas Wesleyan University and works as a social worker in a secondary school. When she first used the solution-focused approach with a parent, she couldn't wait to come to my child and adolescent counseling class so that she could tell everyone what had happened. She relayed to us that she often had a problem getting parents involved at school because they rarely answered the phone or called back; they assumed that if the school called, there was a problem. In the case written by Nicole that follows, she shows how she found an opportunity for a different kind of telephone call and discovered in the process that she could work wonders by using a different kind of approach.

Julie, a middle school student, was sent to my office by one of her teachers. When she arrived, she was crying and very upset. Julie had physical education (PE) second period and still did not have the appropriate clothes. She was worried that she was going to get into trouble again with her teacher. She told me that she had moved here from New Orleans because of Hurricane Katrina, and her mom had planned to get some gym clothes for her last weekend, but her mom was too busy with her new boyfriend.

I asked Julie what she had done during the past few weeks for clothes, and she told me that she had been wearing gym clothes for PE, just not in the right colors. I told her how smart she was to still put on her gym clothes and participate even if the clothes were not the right colors. I asked her what made her decide to still wear them even though she did not have the right colors. She said that she did not want to get in trouble for not dressing properly so she thought that was better than nothing. I told her how wise I thought that she was to do that.

I told her that since she was so good at making decisions, I wondered what she could do that day to avoid being in trouble. She said that she could maybe talk to her PE teacher and explain the situation to her. I told her that I thought that was a great idea. I then asked her what else she could do, and she said she could see if there were any shorts she could borrow from a friend. Once again I praised her on how good she was at solving problems.

She then told me that she wished her mom would buy the shorts this weekend, but with her new boyfriend around so much, she probably won't. She said they never spend time together anymore, and that made her very upset. I asked her what she thought she could do about that, and she did not seem to know. Eventually she said that maybe she could try to talk to her mom and see if that worked. I told her to give it a try and to let me know.

When we finished, Julie still had a sad look on her face, and I asked her if she was okay. She said that she really missed spending time with her mom. I asked her what she would do with her mom if they could spend some time together. She said she would want to go to the park or go shopping. I asked her if there would be a time where she could ask her mom to do that with her, and she said maybe this weekend.

When Julie went to class I called Mom and told her that Julie had just left my office and complimented Mom on what a great daughter she had. I told her how much Julie loved her and how lucky she was that Julie still wanted to spend time with her now that she was in middle school, when most kids prefer their friends. Mom, surprised, said "thank you" and then remarked that lately she had not spent a lot of time with Julie. I asked Mom if she did spend some time with Julie, what she would like to do. She said that she could take her to get some PE clothes because Julie had been asking her to get them for school. I told Mom that she had a great idea.

The next day Julie came into my office smiling from ear to ear. She said that her mom had taken her shopping last night to get her PE clothes and then took her to get her nails done. Since then I have seen Julie in the hall and asked her how things were going. She said things were going really well and that she and her mom have started to spend more time together, like before.

It can really be this simple. It takes so little time. It merely takes perseverance and a belief that when people have an opportunity to see themselves differently, they act differently and respond differently, and the outcome changes.

The Field Guide to Counseling Toward Solutions

Meet the Parents' Needs Too

Working with parents in schools to gain their cooperation means finding out what they want to accomplish for their children first. When their requests seem impossible, the solution-focused school counselor commends them instead of telling them that they can't accommodate their request. The following story is an example.

Tadahisa, a senior in high school, was assigned to me when I began my high school counselor career. I was told by my colleagues that he had a "needy" mom who would be calling me each week: "Beware that she will take up a lot of your time asking questions and trying to bail out Tadahisa." When I talked to Lucy the first time about Tadahisa, I found her to be a loving mom who had been through a lot with her son. Apparently Tadahisa, an only child, had given her a few trying moments in his school career, and she and his dad had been given quite an earful of problems by the school staff. I wondered what she was trying to accomplish by calling me so often, and one day decided to call her as often as she called me, just to chat and tell her how much I enjoyed working with her son. Soon the calls slowed down, and I heard from her only occasionally—until the month before Tadahisa's high school graduation.

Lucy called me, furious and full of questions about a 504 plan, a modification plan often given to students who have learning disabilities. "I want him enrolled in the 504 plan today! He's been ADD all of his life and I can't believe that the schools have never suggested that he be enrolled in that plan. Do you know how hard he and I have struggled with homework all of these years?"

Surprised to hear such a request a scant four weeks prior to her son's graduation, I gathered my thoughts and began to talk to her differently than she expected: "You are right. A 504 plan has modifications and might have been helpful to Tadahisa. But you know, what's even more exciting is that he has made it through without the plan. Just think, he struggled and made it, doing all the work, instead of having it changed or modified to a lower level. That means he has the ability. I'll bet that makes you prouder than ever of him."

For more than a few moments, all I could hear was silence. Then she spoke up: "Thank you. Do you know how rarely I have heard words like that about Tadahisa? Yes, I am proud of him." As she got tearful, we talked more until she felt better about graduation, his leaving for college, and what it would be like with him gone.

A few weeks later, Tadahisa dropped by to tell me that he had gotten into a college a thousand miles from home. With a smile on his face and mine, somehow, I thought it was a good move for both him and his mom.

Pitfalls and Safeguards: Be Very Patient

My early days as a solution-focused school counselor were not always successful, partly because the school staff did not share my passion for the solution-focused approach yet. Also, I had not done the groundwork to support my efforts. This chapter has lots of examples of working with teachers, parents, and teams. Although these cases worked out well, there were earlier ones that taught me important lessons the hard way:

- Be patient. Members of a school staff mean well when they march into your office, frustrated over a student, complaining about a student's performance or attitude. They tend to offer negative descriptions because they are often in a place where they feel helpless and powerless to help a student. Some students today deal with challenging situations: parents in prison, parents who are abusive or abusing drugs, friends who have been murdered in a gang- or drug-related shooting. Some students may not even know who their parents are. These students come to school angry, and they take out their frustrations on their teachers. Be patient with the teacher who goes over and over a situation, and let him know that you appreciate the referral.

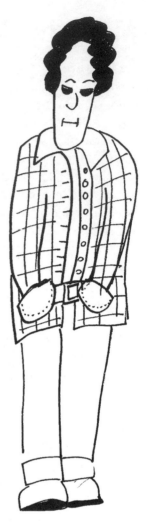

• School teams tend to focus on problems because educators tend to see problems as targets for interventions. That is what they know, and to change their mind-set takes time. It is a paradigm shift for them. Luckily, teachers are easier to educate about the solution-focused model because they don't struggle with other counseling models like trained counselors do. By asking the team if they are willing to try something new and then complimenting them on their willingness to do so, you will gain their trust and confidence. Gradually introduce the solution-focused approach to them, explaining your role as being to help them stay on track with the process. Don't be surprised if they say that your "positive approach" is valuable but not quite applicable to the case that they are discussing. Agree with them, and then explain that it is a chance to look for times when the problem doesn't occur as often. Tell them that you do recognize that it is a different approach, but it is one that your principal endorses and that you are using often.

• Consult with your principal, and let him or her know that trying out these ideas will relieve the assistant principal's position since many of the discipline interventions will be done by teachers in the classroom or hallway rather than through referral. In fact, talk to the assistant principals, and see if they will consider referring simple discipline cases back to the teachers and notify you to assist in the process. Don't worry: that won't overwhelm you once teachers see that they can be competent in solving a variety of situations through the process. Keep both the principal and the vice principal informed and in touch with how the process is going.

Action Plan: Redescribe and Survive

The next time you are asked to see a student whom a parent or team has labeled as "lazy" or a teacher has labeled as "someone who doesn't care," pay attention to your own reaction. Do you suddenly find yourself thinking, "Well, what can I do if the student is lazy or doesn't care?" Realize that thinking in that manner is problem focused, not solution focused. Instead, ask yourself: "How else can I describe this student? When is it that he isn't as lazy or does seem to care slightly?" Then send an e-mail to the teacher and ask these questions. Call the parents, and ask them the same questions. You will effect change two ways by doing this.

First, the parent and teacher will hear a new description of the student, and although they may reject it at first, it will nevertheless have an impact: it will make them think. It may also be hard for them to come up with the answers, but be patient. Calm them by saying, "You know, it is hard to think of times when these behaviors aren't dominating the student, but I would really appreciate your patience with this request. I will check back with you in a few days."

Second, the student will see you working for him, and when you suggest the idea of the new adjective that describes him, watch how his cooperation blossoms.

Chapter Four

Stopping the Special Education Referrals Creatively

Competence, like truth, beauty and contact lenses,
is in the eye of the beholder.

—Laurence J. Peter

On a very cold morning in Davenport, Iowa, I walked into an elementary school for a parent conference. Actually, it was not just any parent conference but a solution-focused parent conversation. The school principal, Bill Long, under instruction from his superintendent, had, with the other ten elementary schools in the district, vowed two years prior that it would not refer children for special education without going through a solution-focused process. That process was composed of a series of meetings labeled as Levels A, B, C, and D. These were the different levels of conversations that used a solution-focused approach to elicit competencies, not deficits, in students who were behind academically or had behavioral challenges, or both. On this particular morning, I was to attend a Level B meeting with Leticia, age ten, a fourth-grade student, and her grandmother, Billee. In the room were seven other educators: each of Leticia's teachers, an associate principal, and the special education teacher-consultant. At one end of the long conference table, Billee and Leticia sat together, gazing at the meeting participants and looking a bit worried. Next to them was the school counselor, ready with her laptop that was cued to a template used for such meetings.

The meeting began with the school counselor's introduction:

Good morning. Thanks for coming, everyone. I know it's early. I promise to have you all to class before school begins at 8:00. We are happy to have Leticia and her grandmother, who wants us to call her Billee, with us today. We are going to have a solution-focused conversation that we think will help to give us some ideas on helping Leticia move up two grade levels in reading.

   This is a Level B meeting which means that for the past six weeks, Leticia, Billee, and Leticia's language arts teacher, Ms. Shoffield, have worked together in a Level A process to raise Leticia's reading level from second grade to fourth grade. Although there has been some progress, Leticia's teacher is still concerned and wanted us to meet so that the group could discuss additional ways to help Leticia. Everyone in this room knows Leticia. Please introduce yourselves to her grandmother.

   As the meeting continued, the school counselor went over the Level A exceptions that had been identified in a parent conference with Billee, Leticia, and her language arts teacher six weeks ago and then asked the teacher to describe Leticia's current success, using a scale. Her teacher described her as a 4 on a scale of 1 to 10, with 10 being at fourth-grade reading level. Afterward the school counselor talked about the protocol for the Level B meeting. She did this while following the Level B: Solution-Focused Conversation template (a reproducible for this template follows). The meeting took thirty minutes.

   After completing the meeting, I had a chance to speak with Billee and Leticia as they left the room. I was curious about how they felt about the meeting. First, I asked them both: "What was it like for you to meet with all of the teachers and staff who are involved with Leticia every day?"

   The grandmother answered:

You know, when I was first called, I thought it would be like most conferences I've been to where you hear what's wrong and what you are going to have to do to make it right. In our case, teachers always thought Leticia was dumb, but like I said today, she is behind in reading because her mother left her in charge of three little siblings younger than her while she went out to deal drugs. Leticia rarely made it to school last year until I took her in. But it was very different today. Instead of deciding to just put her in special ed, they talked about what my granddaughter was doing right. That's a switch. Everybody needs to hear that once in a while, even me! They each seemed to really be concerned.

Leticia answered:

In my last school I couldn't read books in my grade either, so I was always going to tutoring, and I heard people say that I was always behind, and that made me sad. But today it felt like everyone in the room liked me.

With the Level B paperwork completed and printed out, the grandmother took home a copy of the conversation that described what she was to do to help Leticia at home. Each teacher involved with Leticia's school day also received a copy of the paperwork in their mailbox by the end of the day, describing what their role was in the process. The Level B meeting would occur again in three weeks, the date already set, where the participants would again reevaluate the progress that Leticia had made. If some progress was made, the referral would stay at a Level B status until Leticia reached competency in reading. After six to twelve weeks, if there was little progress, the team would decide whether to try six more weeks or refer her on to Level C, which involved contacting the local area education service center for more resources.

Leticia never made it to Level C. Instead, she reached competency that school year and remained in the general education classroom.

Level B: Solution-Focused Conversation

Name: _____ Date: _____

Teacher: _____ Team: _____

Participants present at the meeting:

_____

_____

1. Concern

What concern will this meeting address today?

_____

_____

On a scale of 1 to 10, with 1 being the worst and 10 being completely successful, where is the student currently in regard to the concern? _____

2. Goal setting

What should the student be able to do in order to be more successful in the classroom so that the scaling score increases during the next three weeks?

_____

_____

_____

3. Exception identification

When is this happening slightly already, even in other classrooms and situations at school or outside of school? (Ask staff, parent, and student.)

_____

_____

_____

_____

56

Level B: Solution-Focused Conversation (cont.)

When else in the past has this student been able to increase her academic success on a small scale? What did other teachers or tutors do that worked? (Ask parent and student.)

_____

_____

What was different or helpful in that situation to the student? (Ask the student.)

_____

_____

4. Strategy development

Of these ideas, which ones can we use and adapt to the classroom for the next few weeks? (Identify who will carry out the strategies, and how.)

_____

_____

_____

How will we know, when we meet again in a few weeks, that the scaling score has increased? (What will be happening in the classroom?)

_____

_____

_____

_____

To staff, parent, and student: What was helpful for you today in this conversation?

_____

_____

_____

_____

Next meeting date: _____   Time: _____

Learning to Collaborate Toward Solutions

For the past five years, I have had the pleasure of working as a consultant to the Mississippi Bend Area Education Agency and Davenport Community Schools where an overabundance of special education referrals had concerned the administration. Through a collaborative yet challenging effort, the school district became solution focused primarily in its elementary and intermediate schools, where special education referrals decreased dramatically. The elementary school described at the beginning of this chapter had had more than twenty-five referrals to special education a year prior to the implementation of the solution-focused conversation. By the end of the next year, only two students had been referred.

What caused this drop in referrals? The general education teachers learned to use the exceptions identified in the Level A, B, and C meetings and use their own competencies and area education resources. Although they were not often enthusiastic about the process, once they learned that it could happen and be successful, there was no turning back. Three years prior to the conversation, if Leticia had transferred to the same elementary school and demonstrated the same two-year deficiency in reading, chances are that she would have been immediately referred for a special education assessment. She might have been tested, diagnosed, and placed in special education classes, where she might still remain, away from her peers during reading class until she tested out. Leticia would probably have received some very helpful instruction and modifications that would aim toward raising her reading score, but she would have also missed out on being in the least restrictive environment with her peers. And those students already in special education would have to share their time with a student who did not need as much instruction as they did.

A Different Kind of Spotlight

There is no doubt that special education programs are invaluable for students who have learning disabilities and deficits. However, it is those students who deserve the spotlight, not students who are simply behind and challenging to teach. Think how much better it would be if special education teachers could devote more time to those truly in need, while the general education teachers learned some useful techniques from special education teachers, area education service centers, and their peers to use with students who are struggling. And imagine the impact on the students.

Today in Davenport, not only are elementary and middle schools still adhering to this process (it has become district policy), but many of their staff meetings and faculty meetings in these lower grades are also facilitated with a solution-focused process. The meetings start with a goal; then they develop exceptions that turn into strategies and then tasks. Faculty members now hear the words *solution focused* and see the process as an efficient one. But it took time, support from the administration, and a charge from the superintendent to make it mandatory. The process has now become a part of the school culture. It has also spread to the secondary campuses, where solution-focused staff meetings and student collaboration on success take place often.

How Do You Spell Success?

Many people believe that the term *solution focused* means "being positive" or "student friendly," particularly in the high school setting. Davenport took a different approach: Many of the students who, prior to the implementation of the solution-focused program, might have been placed in special education are now staying in the regular education classrooms on all grade levels. The teachers and students have different kinds of conversations than in the past—the kind that lead to solutions rather than confrontations and threats. In fact, in Davenport's Central High School, a solution-focused interventionist meets regularly with teachers who are concerned about particular students. The meeting may begin with complaints and concerns, but the solution-focused interventionist guides the teachers in the direction of solutions so that when the meeting is over, the strategies begin.

How a New Mind-set Is Created

Consider this story. Once upon a time, a group of fine teachers wanted their classrooms to be teachable and manageable. Yet they failed to realize all of their own abilities and competencies because the administration took care of all of their referrals, dealt with the students, referred them for special education, and the story ended happily—for the teachers, but not necessarily for the students. Eventually these teachers, when called on to perform way above the normal scope of their competence by reteaching those with deficiencies, became angry at the administration. How dare they expect such exceptional attention for a student who surely needed special education! What were they supposed to do? Become miracle workers? What did they know about working with a student who had a learning problem? It just wasn't within their ability to know what to try next.

I sat in a sixth-grade team meeting in an intermediate school in Davenport three years after we implemented the solution-focused Level A, B C, and D meetings to listen to such a group of teachers talk about Larry, a sixth grader who had poor reading comprehension skills:

> TEAM LEADER: We have to discuss Larry Smith. He is failing language arts and social studies because he has trouble with his comprehension. Ms. Jones, you are his language arts teacher. How is Larry doing?
>
> MS. JONES: Not well, really. He seems to do well in math and science because he can work well in pairs, and when he does, he can pass. But give him a book to read or a chapter to summarize, and he's lost.
>
> TEAM LEADER: Well, we all know that in the past if we saw a student like Larry struggle, we would request some testing. But since we know we can't do that before starting the level process, I'm not sure what to do next.

At that time, my role was to be a consultant to intermediate teams such as this one. In the intermediate school, the process started with the teams, and if the team couldn't reach consensus and some success, they proceeded to the level in the process. I remember vividly the frustrated and partly angry looks on the faces of the team teachers. With this in mind, I said, "You are all trying so hard, and that's plain to see. But I happen to believe that you have some abilities to help Larry, maybe even more than you do. So let's say if your paycheck depended on Larry's getting some different kinds of help to help him comprehend better just for the next grading period, what would you come up with?"

After a few minutes of silence, the conversation began again.

MR. LIVINGSTON: Well, what is it about pairs that helps him in science and math? I am his computer teacher, and he does fine in my class on his own.

MS. CLIFFORD: I have him in science, and if he gets stuck, he has a buddy to help him. What I've always done is match him with a student who reads well and stays on task. Larry can do the work. I've seen it. He just has a hard time reading and remembering.

MR. JACKSON: My wife teaches elementary school across the street. I remember once that she had a student who was one grade level behind in reading, and what she and another teacher did was team her up with a younger student in a lower grade and have her read to the student several times a week. The student was told that after the reading, she had to explain to the student what the reading was about. They had pretty good success. The student thought it was a real privilege to read to a younger student, and she actually behaved better in class. Seemed to work.

MS. JONES: So are you saying that perhaps pairing up Larry with a younger student might be a plan?

TEAM LEADER: It sounds like an idea.

MR. JACKSON: I have a morning break around 10:00 each day. What if I walked Larry across the street to read with a student? I could ask my wife whom she would recommend.

And so the saga of Larry's reading skills began to take a different shape. When forced to think of an alternative way to reach him, the teachers creatively found a way to address his reading skills. This type of intervention began happening all over the school district. Teachers tried new ideas, students got better, and teachers felt competent.

Becoming Solution Focused

It isn't easy for Kermit the Frog to be green, and it isn't easy for many educators to become solution focused. Most teachers want things to stay as they always have been. However, if a district is committed to making a difference for students in the area and to keeping them in the least restricted environment, implementing the approach is a great start. In Davenport, it was the charge to do something different that catapulted the district into change and made its employees more competent than ever before. As a result, the district became more diverse in its approach to helping students succeed, and morale grew.

The move toward a solution-focused conversation began with the administration. Those in charge learned about the solution-focused approach from the Mississippi Bend Area Education Agency; they studied it carefully and formed study groups to discuss the process. They found the approach to have just the right amount of solution-finding resources that they needed. They had read my book, *Counseling Toward Solutions* (1994, 2008), and liked the approach of the solution-focused conversation with students and parents. They attended several workshops that I presented to them in Davenport and talked in task force meetings with the superintendent. Once top administrative staff embraced the approach, the next step was to take it to the principals. They elected a chair, who then designated certain staff members to monitor and coach certain schools. Their thinking was that if the principals embraced the idea, the rest of the staff could learn to do the process through training. The school counselor would be a key player throughout that process.

The principals were at first ambivalent about changing the process that they already knew how to do. Convincing them of the need for a new approach took training them in the solution-focused model and practicing the model in role plays. It took more explanations of how the model could work with a wide variety of learning issues. They had to understand it in language that they knew. They were taught how the model was different from a problem-focused approach. Then they were asked to commit to do it. This commitment meant that I would do site visits every two to three months to follow up with the principals on what was expected. The principals tried to get staff on board, and that meant I came to train staff in the model in after-school training sessions several times. I sat in on their team meetings, met with school counselors and principals, and monitored the progress.

The Ultimate Charge

The administrative staff gave the principals a charge in August of the second year of training:

> We want you to go back to your schools and, along with your school counselor, go through your special education students, look at why they were referred and do a Level A and Level B meeting on those students. See if they belong in special education. No new referrals are to be made unless they follow the Level A and Level B process. When you begin and complete a Level A, B, and C process, we ask that you send us a copy of the meeting at the main office.

To change a system takes time. There was anxiety in Davenport about a new process. But they took their charge to their buildings and their staff. They studied the Level A, B, and C forms that were given to them and modified them to fit their own schools. For three more years, I would appear every three months or so to hear about how the process was working. In the end, things fell into a different place, as systems theory states it will. When some administrators had difficulty implementing the process, the others encouraged them and monitored them, offering assistance and support. The message was clear, and Davenport Community Schools never stopped sending it.

When all of the dust settled, the district had in place a process that seemed to work for students, parents, and even teachers. When the special education referrals dropped, those in charge decided that all student interventions should be handled in the same manner. Davenport is to be saluted for a job well done!

The Solution-Focused Intervention Process

The material in this section, written by the Mississippi Bend Area Education Agency (AEA) in Bettendorf, Iowa, in August 2000, describes its solution-focused program.

Guiding Philosophy

All children should be educated in the least restrictive environment (LRE). When concerns regarding student progress are identified, initial efforts will attempt to identify student and system strengths and exceptions to problems in order to design interventions within general education.

Underlying Assumptions

The *solution-focused intervention process* is a competency-based model consistent with the following assumptions:

- Solution-focused language drives the intervention planning process. Questions play a powerful role in solution-focused conversations.
- Focusing on the positive, on solutions, and on present and future goals facilitates change in the desired direction.
- Students, parents, and teachers have the resources to resolve their concerns, and solutions are achievable when they define their own goals.
- Change is constant. A small change in one part of a system is frequently all that is necessary to effect change in other parts of the system. Complex problems do not necessitate complex solutions.
- If an intervention works, do more of the same. If an intervention does not work, do something different. Solutions to current concerns develop from past successes.
- Exceptions, those times when the concerns or problems are not occurring, guide us to potential solutions.

Description of the Model

This model involves collaboration among students, parents, instructional staff and AEA staff in an ongoing search for solutions by clarifying student strengths and needs, looking for exceptions to the problem/issues, and designing interventions based on student and system strengths/abilities. Evaluation and assessment activities are guided by student-specific questions. Clarification of student needs, strengths, and goals for the design of intervention plans may, as needed, encompass assessment of system, home, community, and individual-centered variables. Subsequent intervention plans may then address changes in any of these variables. Only after general education–based interventions have been exhausted or when the interventions exceed the capacity of general education will special education be considered as a possible intervention. The previous dichotomy of special and general education should become more blurred as all education services are increasingly blended to assist students in the least restrictive environment possible.

The *solution-focused intervention process* has four levels. These levels fall into three distinct types of intervention:

Level A—Initial Intervention

Levels B and C—Collaborative Interventions

Level D—Full and Individual Evaluation

These levels alone are not the only component of the *solution-focused intervention process*. These levels provide a structure; however, the use of solution-focused language allows for the tapping of unrealized capacities for those involved in the process. The expectation is that data collection and progress monitoring also will occur throughout all four levels of the *solution-focused intervention process*.

The use of solution-focused language is vital to the process. Examples of solution-focused language include questions that identify those times when the presenting concerns do not occur or are less intense, questions that encourage visualization of a future without the problem, questions that conceptualize the concern in less pathological terms, and questions that solicit goal setting.

The initial intervention, Level A, focuses on the interactions among the student, the parent(s), and the teacher(s) to find solutions. Collaborative interventions, Levels B and C, are designed to occur in general education and may indirectly or directly involve assistance from the AEA. Full and individual evaluation, Level D, involves assessment for special education services when it is deemed to be a viable and necessary alternative to general education *after* time has been given to working through the process of Levels A, B, and C. This may take over a semester to accomplish, giving the student and staff ample opportunity to explore different approaches to teaching and learning. Following is an explanation of how the levels work together and on the following pages are samples of templates for Levels A and C.

For Level D, the special education referral, use your current district form for referral and add copies of Level A, B, and C for use during the IEP [Individualized Education Plan].

Solution-Focused Intervention Process

LEVEL A: Concern about individual's performance is expressed by teachers, parents, or individual. If the process in Level A works to accomplish individual goals, further referral to next level is unnecessary. If goals are not met, go to next level.

LEVEL B: Request for teacher assistance team for collaboration about individual concerns. Team may include AEA staff, teachers, parents, administrators. If the process in Level B works to accomplish individual goals, further referral to next level is unnecessary. If goals are not met within a time frame designated by team, a referral is made to next level.

LEVEL C: Request for additional support services from AEA staff by teachers, parents, and administration. Support may come in the form of health, hearing, vision screening, developmental milestones, and monitoring. Additional interventions are agreed upon through the Level C process and if progress is obtained, this process continues indefinitely per team approval. If not, a consent for a full and individual evaluation for consideration of special education services is obtained.

LEVEL D: School counselor reviews previous assessments/interventions from previous level meetings, conducts necessary assessments per special education evaluation. If individual is entitled to special education services due to meeting guidelines for standard disability categories or noncategories, an IEP will be developed with parental input and will be implemented. An annual review will be conducted and a 3-year reevaluation will be scheduled.

Level A: Solution-Focused Conversation

Name: _____ Date: _____

Advisory Teacher: _____ Team: _____

Participants present at the meeting: (parent, teacher, and student)

_____

_____

1. Concern

What concern will this meeting address today?

Teacher: _____

Parent: _____

On a scale of 1–10, with 1 being the worst and 10 being completely successful, where is the student currently in regard to the concern? _____

2. Goal setting

What will the student be doing in the classroom over the next few weeks so that the scaling score increases and our concern decreases?

_____

_____

3. Exception identification

When is this happening slightly already, even in other classrooms and situations at school? (Ask for student and parent answers.)

_____

_____

Where else have some of these actions happened before, in other grade levels or situations outside of school? (Ask for student and parent answers.)

_____

_____

Level A: Solution-Focused Conversation (cont.)

What was different or helpful in those situations?

_____

_____

4. Strategy development

Of these ideas, which ones can we use and adapt in the classroom and at home for the next few weeks? (Identify by who and how the strategies will be carried out.)

_____

_____

_____

_____

How will we know, when we meet again in a few weeks, that things are improving? What will we see happening, specifically?

_____

_____

_____

_____

To parent and student: What was helpful for you today in this conversation?

_____

_____

_____

_____

Next meeting date: _____   Time: _____

Level C: Solution-Focused Conversation

Name: _____ Date: _____

Advisory Teacher: _____ Team: _____

Participants present at the meeting:

_____

_____

1. Concern

What concern will this meeting address today?

_____

_____

On a scale of 1–10, with 1 being the worst and 10 being completely successful, where is the student currently in regard to the concern? _____

2. Goal setting

What should the student be able to do in order to be more successful in the classroom so that the scaling score increases during the next three weeks?

_____

_____

3. Exception identification

When is this happening slightly already, even in other classrooms and situations at school?

_____

_____

_____

What current Level A and B strategies have assisted the student in raising the scaling score?

_____

_____

Level C: Solution-Focused Conversation (cont.)

When else in the past has this student been able to increase academic success on a small scale?

_____

_____

What was different or helpful in that situation?

_____

_____

4. Strategy development

Which additional resources (vision, hearing, developmental milestone assessment, etc.) does the team feel might be helpful in order to assist the student in being more successful?

_____

_____

What does the team need or expect to happen as a result of resource involvement?

_____

_____

How will we know, when we meet again in three weeks, that the resource interventions have been helpful?

_____

_____

To staff, resource staff, parent, and student: What was helpful for you today in this conversation?

_____

_____

Next meeting date: _____ Time: _____

IDEA and No Child Left Behind

As a school counselor, you have probably encountered the Individuals with Disabilities Education Act, which closely works together with the No Child Left Behind Act. The solution-focused intervention process described in this chapter is supportive of the recommendations made by Congress in that:

- Students are placed in the least restrictive environment to receive additional services by staff and support staff.

- Parents are included in the process of their child's education and are seen as a resource.

- Staff are trained to offer more services and strategies that support the needs of students who need additional learning situations.

- It is believed that students should learn with their peers unless they show, through the Level A, B, and C process, that their individual needs surpass that which the classroom teacher can provide.

- Support staff from local area education agencies can assist the regular classroom teacher with student learning, allowing the student to stay in the general education classroom.

- Exceptions, identified by staff, parents, and support staff, are key elements in the solution-focused intervention process in that they raise and stabilize expectations of general education teachers toward their students.

For more information, visit the Web site of the U.S. Department of Education (www.ed.gov).

New Expectations, New Results

The solution-focused intervention process described in this chapter offers children and adolescents an opportunity to stay in the general education classroom, experience learning with their peers, and exceed current expectations that lead to success. It should be noted that in addition to using the Level A, B, and C process with general education, the special education teachers in Davenport also began to use the language of the process with their students and parents, particularly when they were developing the solution-focused individualized education program, introduced in Chapter Six of this Field Guide. Many of the special education teachers found that the language was not only a fresh approach to promoting competency, but also helped to promote confidence in the students whose scaling score increased. Parents liked the approach since the language gave them hope for their children.

The process places extra expectations on teachers and staff to develop new skills and patience in teaching children and adolescents who struggle in the regular classroom. This is perhaps the biggest challenge, yet if the program is implemented firmly and expectations of teachers are made contractually, the result will be a faculty that grows enormously in its capacities. This nonpathological approach creates an atmosphere in which teachers ask what they will do to reach students rather than say why they can't reach those students. And the winner? Everyone.

Pitfalls and Safeguards: Staying on Track and Liking It

A fundamental concept of project development, implementation, and success is buy-in (see Chapter Two). The job of solution-focused school counselors is to create an atmosphere where staff, students, parents, and administration have opportunities to be confident and competent. To do that takes not only expertise but consistent follow-up and support from the principal.

Many projects fail when staff are told to do something new without any kind of reward to them personally. Although the project may sound great, the idea of one more project or a different way of doing something is not typically well received by a hard-working faculty. Instead, they respond in these ways: "I don't have any time already," "When do you expect us to do this?" and "When will the student or parent become more responsible?"

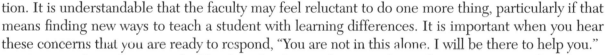

These are legitimate concerns from a staff who may feel overwhelmed with yet another new expectation. It is understandable that the faculty may feel reluctant to do one more thing, particularly if that means finding new ways to teach a student with learning differences. It is important when you hear these concerns that you are ready to respond, "You are not in this alone. I will be there to help you."

In my early work, I was asked by the school counselor or guidance director to approach and train staff so that teachers had a new approach to use with challenging students or with special education referrals. Although some staffs seemed interested, the project rarely took off because no one "made them do it." However, when I was approached by a principal who embraced the idea and introduced me as a consultant with an important message that he or she expected to be carried out, the program had a better chance. It was in those schools, such as Davenport, that the process worked.

As you begin the process with the action plan that follows, make sure that the principal is on board and committed. Chances are that he or she would like to know that special education referrals are reduced in the school as a result. Knowledge that the school is adhering closely to both the Individuals with Disabilities Education Act and No Child Left Behind Act is also appealing. Take your time to accomplish this important piece, and the project will have a better chance of working.

Action Plan: Take on a New Focus

The following steps have been identified as quite helpful when implementing most new projects in schools. They are the result of my experiences as a consultant and are steps that I have identified as the ones that work with staff:

1. Meet with the principal and associate principal. Lend them this book, and ask them to read Chapter Two. Explain your part in the process. Also provide a copy of Chapter Two to the

administrator, which describes how you will work with the staff. Answer as many questions that the principal may have until he or she is supportive of the process for the students.

2. At the next faculty meeting, ask for the principal to introduce you and allow you to introduce the Level A, B, and C meetings. Discuss the current numbers of special education students. Ask the principal to endorse the program to the faculty as a means of reducing the numbers and increasing student competency. Ask him or her to tell the faculty that he or she expects their support as of the date that the program begins.

3. As you talk to the faculty, pass out the Level A Solution-Focused Conversation form, and talk through it with the faculty. Mention that it is simply a new format to follow to find solutions. Tell them that during the next few weeks (or months, or whatever the schedule is), they will be attending brief training sessions before or after school to learn about the solution-focused intervention process.

4. Tell them that they are not alone. You are a major player in this process, which promises not only to help students but to help teachers identify ways to reach students and achieve classroom management that works for everyone.

5. Follow through. Begin the process on the designated day. Conduct the training on convenient days (never Fridays), provide refreshments (ask the Parent-Teacher Association to help), and make the sessions fun. Use Chapter Two, on training staff, as a guide for stimulating the thinking of your teachers and staff. Thank them through e-mails.

Chapter Five

Combining Your Resources

Solution-Focused Support Groups

Applying solution-focused ideas to groups in elementary and secondary schools simplifies and enriches the process in groups, cuts back on unproductive complaining and story telling, and releases the school counselor from solving the problem. The students have the opportunity to tell their story initially and are then encouraged to switch directions from a problem focus to looking for competencies within themselves and others. Instead of just venting and complaining about teachers, parents, or friends, students leave with "exceptions" to their problem, contributed by group members and the school counselor. Instead of the groups' being described as "problem-student groups," the groups might be described as:

- An opportunity for students to discover for themselves and from group members how they might have solved their problems before
- A time to develop a plan that makes the problem less of a problem and places the student in charge of the solution
- A time to share successes and feel supported by other group members

Solution-Focused Group Counseling

Most school counselors run support groups in their schools on specific topics, such as divorce, anger, friendship, substance abuse, sexual abuse, sadness and loss, and any other common topic or issues that may surface throughout the year. These groups are often held weekly in elementary and secondary schools. When I facilitated groups in different grade levels, I tried to conduct the groups for thirty minutes at the elementary schools and forty-five minutes at the secondary schools. I also found it helpful and respectful to teachers to conduct the groups during the last part of the class period so that students could gain instruction at the first part and complete their work later. Each week the group was held at a different time so that the students did not miss out on class time in any one class too often.

Many school counselors are also required to provide groups for issues such as social skills and test-taking skills. Typical support groups in elementary and middle schools have a curriculum with activities designed to bring out feelings and issues that bother students and provide them with a problem-solving model. The group serves as a sounding board and support system to students. These groups are more instructive and "taught" than they are process oriented. Students tend to like the activities and participate as they would during a class. If curriculum-based groups are chosen, they can be adapted toward the solution-focused model when the school counselor takes a back seat and allows the students to become the expert in the activities. The model can also be incorporated by using the following types of questions after the activity:

"What did you think about the activity we just did?"

"What did you notice about your group members that impressed you?"

"How will these ideas help you with your [issue] tomorrow?"

"Tell us each a small step that you can take to begin doing that."

"What will you tell yourself that has worked before?"

Basic Guidelines for Group Counseling

Adapting the solution-focused approach to group counseling in schools means following some basic ideas similar to those presented earlier in this book (adapted from Metcalf, 1998).

1. Keep the group nonpathological, redescribing problems to open up possibilities for each group member.

One of the easiest ways to keep the group solution focused rather than problem focused is to have students name their group. There is quite a different message conveyed when a group named The Angry Student Group instead calls itself Anger Managers or when The Very Depressed Group becomes the Depression Busters group. When a school counselor in Plano, Texas, gathered female middle school students who had a tendency to fight with their mothers, the group began with a griping session and said they wanted to name their group the We Hate Our Mothers Group. The school counselor discouraged such a name, but instead  of putting the girls down, he suggested that they talk about what the group was to try and accomplish. Eventually, with that concept in mind, the group became To Mother with Love.

2. Focus on exceptions to problems that are discussed and displayed in group interactions. Notice a group member's competency in the group process, and mention what you notice, gathering other group members' thoughts on your discovery.

I have often mused at the students sent to Anger Managers groups who come in polite and friendly, happy to be there. I sometimes voice my curiosity saying, "You know, you all look fine to me. I don't see any anger anywhere!" This often brings a smile to the faces of the group members, who then talk about the reasons that they were referred. Then the group can continue by addressing these topics:

"What is different about the times when you do not feel angry?"

"Let's discuss the ways that you have each resisted the urge to let anger take over at times."

"Before we stop, what have you noticed about each other as we spoke together today?"

Another way to use exceptions is to make a list of the situations and techniques the members use to fight anger, overcome depression, or cope better. For children, drawings can be made of the problem and the solution. They can then hold up the picture and talk about what happens when the problem, rather than the solution, is around. The focus on exceptions changes the direction of the group so that the children become more aware of their own solutions.

---

3. Avoid any tendency to promote insight. Instead, focus on group members' ability to survive the situation.

In schools, searching for insight takes time, something that school counselors rarely have enough of. Holding the focus in group counseling on coping skills and what works and does not work keeps the group out of discussing how terrible things are. Naturally there will be times when a group member has a tough day or week and wants to talk—and probably needs to talk. As the group listens and empathizes, the solution-focused school counselor listens as well and eventually tries to encourage the student to talk about what he or she wants to be different.

---

4. Attempt to see the group members as people who have complaints about their lives, not as persons with symptoms.

In solution-focused group counseling, the client's experience of hearing that he or she has abilities and coping mechanisms is a relief— a relief that can evolve into positive solutions. Begin thinking of yourself as a stage director, helping actors stand in places on a stage where their talents are best noticed and used. When you give competency-based statements to those students, they can be coaxed out of old roles into new roles.

The following exercise is fun for group counseling in middle school or high school. It involves watching a movie such as *Mean Girls,* where one person is put down for not fitting in with a peer group.

Divide your group into two. Tell the students that you will all be watching an excerpt of *Mean Girls* where Lindsay Lohan has just met the preppy students who seem to own their own table in the lunchroom. Ask one group to watch for all of the problems with the interactions and the other members to watch for the strengths of the actors. After viewing the movie, draw a line down the center of a whiteboard and label one side "strengths" and the other "weaknesses." Ask the two sides to give their descriptions, and at the end notice which side has more listed. Discuss how easy it is to label problems and how difficult it can be to identify strengths during chaotic times. Then ask, "If we brought these actors in for consultation with us, which descriptions would give them direction to make changes in their lives that are more satisfying? Why?"

---

5. Remember that complicated, complex problems do not necessarily require complex solutions. Ask the miracle question to help students see beyond their current issues and help them to understand the meaning of their miracle.

This is the miracle question: "Suppose you woke up tomorrow and found that a miracle had happened in your life. What would be different? What would that do for you? How could you begin achieving that on a very small scale, on your own, as an experiment, just for the next week? How would these new behaviors make a difference in your life?"

Talk about how the miracle (refer instead to a magic wand for elementary and middle school students) gives students a respite from their problem and allows them to dream of a time when life goes better. It also gives the solution-focused counselor an idea of what the students' goals and needs are.

Step into each student's worldview to lower resistance. Be respectful of the actions and behaviors that the student has tried in order to solve his or her problem. See these attempts as immature yet meaningful strategies that simply did not work for them.

Ask group members to discuss how their behaviors offer comfort or relief, help to lower resistance, and help them to feel understood. As they identify with each other's experiences, asking other group members for their ideas regarding more positive behaviors that would be less harmful (or illegal) begins a brainstorming session that leads to exception identification. This construction of new, alternative behaviors gives students an additional repertoire of strategies to try for short lengths of time, such as one day, one week, or even just one afternoon. It also keeps them connected with the school counselor, who doesn't come across as an official who aims to stop their drinking, drug use, or negative behaviors using criticism or lecture. Instead, the solution-focused school counselor sees the student's actions as worrisome and conveys that concern to the student, but also acknowledges that the actions had a purpose.

---

6. Focus only on the possible and changeable. Assist students with thinking more specifically and less emotionally when setting goals for group therapy.

When students talk about their problems in group counseling, they often talk about what they don't want to happen anymore. This concept is important to the student, but such a statement cannot be a goal. It is more helpful to assist the student in focusing on what he or she does wants instead. The role of the solution-focused school counselor is to keep helping the student to process the goal until it becomes a visible goal.

The Field Guide to Counseling Toward Solutions

To help them arrive at such a goal, the counselor can ask, "When you are happier someday, what would the group be seeing you do differently?" After students describe their new actions, encourage their peers to list other behaviors that would indicate that happiness was occurring in that student's life.

---

7. Go slowly. Encourage students to ease into solutions gradually. Help them see each new strategy as an experiment that cannot fail or guarantee success. Whatever happens as a result of the attempt is simply an experiment toward change.

When you suggest keeping the future resolution of problems to a limited and brief time frame, students often feel relieved that they are not required to make huge changes overnight. For example, parents who ground their adolescent daughter for the entire school year sometimes stifle any motivation on the daughter's part to improve, and typically the grounding is eventually lifted. As one adolescent reminded me once, "When parents ground you forever, it doesn't give you any reason to get better. Instead you just think, well, I might as well misbehave again. How much worse can it get?"

Using the scaling question to gauge where the students are in regard to solving their problems is very helpful. As each group member defines his or her place on the scale, an atmosphere of competition develops. Before the group session ends, it is helpful to ask the students where they want to be by the next meeting and what they will have to do to get there. Again, this promotes a healthy competition and makes students think about how to change their behavior.

Past Problems Are in the Past

Solution-focused school counselors do not need vast background information on students they work with or understand how things became so difficult for students in order to run a group effectively. In fact, many school districts today discourage counselors from probing into a student's life outside school. The group leader allows the respect and distance that may be appropriate yet stays consistent, focusing on solutions. A counselor can elicit sufficient information for group discussions by simply asking:

"Briefly, what do you think we really need to know about you?"

"What would you say is the bottom line of your concern?"

"What finally happened so that you decided to come here and make changes?"

Sometimes a student will insist on telling war stories. It is important to listen for a sufficient amount of time (varying with each student) and then say that this group is different. Although the group members are interested in hearing about these experiences and are honored that the new member is so trusting in them, it's time to talk about moving away from the problem to a time when things will be better.

Make the Group Exceptional

The solution-focused school counselor listens creatively for exceptions, or times when the problem is not as invasive in the lives of the students. Looking at exceptions to problems is a different approach, but students will catch on to their "exceptional abilities to see themselves differently," especially if the counselor appears curious in the questioning of their success. Be aware of and notice if the problem bothers the students during the group sessions. Assume that things will be better. Ask them directly how they have managed to keep the problem under control during group time. Then ask, "When else today have you been this successful?" If a student can't remember, ask the group.

The Role of the Solution-Focused Group Counselor

The assumptions held by the group leader are vital to the success of the solution-focused group. Your expertise and experience with your students will assist you in developing your own solution-focused questions for various specialty groups. Notice the individual student personalities, the language that the students use, what they need to stay on a subject, and your own resourcefulness and experience in accomplishing that goal. Some students may need to write down ideas, draw ideas, or relate them metaphorically. Your resourcefulness will encourage your students to be resourceful as well.

A solution-focused school counselor who runs the group employing the following assumptions will probably influence the group members to complain less and be more responsible for their individual changes. The group leader assists the group members in seeing their problems as solvable because he or she believes:

- People are competent.
- Change is inevitable.
- Exceptions to the problem exist.
- Change takes time.
- Focusing on solutions is more productive than focusing on problems.

The role of the counselor here is to create an environment in which students can discover and experience their competencies within the group. Some group leaders take an active part in activating "solution talk" through questions for each week or dealing with specific issues. The leader may redescribe the problem alone or collaboratively with the group, and ask the students to talk about it differently, helping them see the problem as helpful through this redescription. Normalizing and dissolving feelings of failure can be accomplished by asking group members to watch other group members during the group time or during the week in school and notice when the troubling problems are not as influential.

The solution-focused school counselor's primary goal is to assist the students in discovering when the difficulty is less of a problem in their lives. One helpful way to begin the first group session is to ask, "What's something you are really good at?" This is an intriguing way of getting to know the resources of the group members. The resources can even be written on a whiteboard and kept during the semester.

As a school counselor using the solution-focused approach, your job just became much easier. You now have group members who can become your co-counselors; your job is to keep the group moving in a direction that keeps blaming out of the process and promotes change. The following steps, adapted from *Solution Focused Group Therapy* (Metcalf, 1998), will help to make this happen:

1. **Set the mood for focusing on solutions.** Ask each student, "As you introduce yourself, give us a brief idea as to why you are here, and tell us what you think we should know." If a student was sent to the group, ask, "What will [the teacher] probably say he or she needs to see you doing differently so that you can stop coming here?"

2. **Suggest goal setting.** Ask, "What will be going on in the future that will tell you and each of us that things are better for you?" If the student describes what others will be doing and forgets to focus on his or her own goal or behavior, help by asking specific questions such as this one: "What will you be doing in that picture?"

3. **Search for exceptions to the problem.** Say, "I've been listening to all of you talk about the reasons that you are here today. Your situations sound quite challenging, and I admire you all for coming here to make things better. Just for a change of pace, let's talk about those times before the problem started. What was going better then?" Then follow up with these questions:

"How did you do that?"

"Where were you?"

"Who was there?"

"How did that keep the problem smaller?"

"What were you thinking about yourself when you were acting differently?"

4. **Encourage motivation.** Say, "Someday, when the problem that brought all of you to group is less of a problem, what will you each get to do more of?" Then follow up with: "As you listen to your peers, is there someone in our group whom you think ought to do something different just for the next week?" and "As we have talked today, who noticed someone who did something different in group that you liked?"

5. **Assist the students with task development.** When goals have been set, ask, "You have all told me some great ideas by describing to me the times when the problem bothers you less. Let's now talk about what you think you might do until we meet again to keep these problems smaller." If goals have not been set, ask, "As we stop today, I would like each of you to watch your day-to-day activities closely until we meet again and notice when your situations are not bothering you as often. Keep track of these exceptions, and bring them with you next time."

Staying on Course with Solutions

When solution-focused ideas are added to groups, the process includes looking for exceptions, doing something different, finding out what is working, and celebrating success. These ingredients become part of a successful group process, making the group more productive and not as problem focused. The group continues throughout its designated course by searching for and identifying exceptions to the problems concerning the group members, which offer solutions toward the designated goal. The group process uses basically the same format as individual and teacher-student conferences.

The questions flow similarly around defining the goal of the student, identifying exceptions to the problem, and developing a task. The use of the miracle question (de Shazer, 1985) as a group topic is helpful in focusing the group members on what they will be doing when the problem is solved: "If you each woke up tomorrow and discovered that a miracle had occurred overnight, what would be different as you went through your day that would tell you things were better for you?"

Developing Goals

The goal of the group is to empower students to solve their own problems. Goals are set early in the group by the individual members and are limited to specific behaviors that each student desires. In other words, the group is not a place to complain about someone else. Should a student want things to be better for him or her and a parent, friend, or teacher, the goal will be stated in terms of what the student might do to change the interaction. A solution-focused assumption is that there is a ripple effect: if one person changes, the interactions eventually must change since the behaviors will not be the same. The leader helps this goal description stay solution focused by asking questions such as these:

"If we followed you around with a video camera on the day you meet your goal and you point out to all of us that life is better, what do you think we will see you doing?"

"You know, I'll bet you've talked a lot about this problem already. Let me suggest that we talk differently about this subject for a few minutes. How would you like things to be someday when the problem doesn't bother you as much?"

The Group Theme

Terry Walkup, a counselor in Plano, Texas, passes out manila file folders to his students as he begins new groups each school year. He gives each member an individual diary to place inside the folder and stores the folders in a confidential file cabinet in his office. (A reproducible Individual Diary sheet follows.) This is a useful and inexpensive idea for keeping track of student success and documenting efficiently in schools. He asks the students to write down their goals, reasons for coming to the group, and uses a scale of 1 to 10, with 1 meaning "I am in control" and 10 meaning "The problem is in control."

Terry asks the students to mark on the scale where they see themselves in regard to their problem as they begin the group sessions. Each week, he begins the session by asking where the student is on the scale in regard to his or her problem and has them circle this new position on the scale they have drawn on their file folder. He then asks them to write down how they accomplished the move. He ends the session by asking, "Where would you like to be when we see you again?" By asking the student "How will you do that?" he assumes change will occur and conveys that assumption to the students.

Individual Diary

Name of Group: _____

My Name: _____

My reason for coming here:

_____

_____

I will know when things are better for me when I am able to:

_____

_____

On the scale below, if 1 = your problems are in complete control of you, and 10 = you are in complete control of your problems, circle where you are today:

1   2   3   4   5   6   7   8   9   10

Group Day 1

Where are you today on the scale? _____

What did you discover today about yourself that will help you move to a different point?

_____

_____

Group Day 2

Where are you today on the scale? _____

What did you discover today about yourself that will help you move to a different point?

_____

_____

Individual Diary (cont.)

Group Day 3

Where are you today on the scale? _____

What did you discover today about yourself that will help you move to a different point?

_____

_____

Group Day 4

Where are you today on the scale? _____

What did you discover today about yourself that will help you move to a different point?

_____

_____

Group Day 5

Where are you today on the scale? _____

What did you discover today about yourself that will help you move to a different point?

_____

_____

Group Day 6

Where are you today on the scale? _____

What did you discover today about yourself that will help you move to a different point?

_____

_____

To Mother with Love Group

Several middle school girls were referred to Terry Walkup by teachers who were concerned about the students' grades, self-esteem, and comments about their negative relationships with their mothers. As he began the group, the members wanted to name the group "We Hate Our Mothers Group." Terry assured them that group time was not going to be about how they hated their mothers, for he was certain that they had already had plenty of discussion on that issue. Instead, he described to them that this was going to be a group where they learned to like, or at least make peace with, their mothers. This simple explanation seemed to work: the members renamed the group "To Mother with Love." Terry said that the renaming of the group set a new context for the girls to begin thinking differently about their mothers.

Terry developed a list of questions from solution-focused ideas to assist the students in their dilemma of hating their mothers. He asked the students to focus on exceptions to the problem and on times when the problem did not interfere in their lives. Terry perceived the students' concerns, and his preparation for the group consisted of questions that would steer them in a more solution-focused direction:

1. Someday when you and your mom begin to get along, what will be better?
2. What will you get to do when the problem isn't there?
3. When in the past has the problem not interfered?
4. On a scale of 1 to 10, where were you when you came in today? Where would you like to be next week?
5. What do you know now about your successes in the past that will help you achieve your goal?

He also devised questions for future sessions:

1. What's going better this week? How have you done that?
2. If I asked your mom what was better, what would she tell me? Stay specific.

Other Ideas for Naming Groups

Group counseling often requires a theme for the group, such as behavioral issues, sibling rivalry, anger, chemical management, or sexual abuse survivor groups, students of divorced families, and educational issues such as study skills. However, becoming solution focused in groups means using words that promote possibilities because these groups focus on competencies. Students enjoy naming their group, so encouraging them to name it with a solution focus is particularly helpful in creating a competent environment. The following group names and their membership are ways of redescribing small groups with a solution focus:

The Anger Managers: A group for elementary students who deal with their own anger or fighting with other students. The group name can be changed to Anger Management for junior high and high school students.

Homework Hustlers: A study skills group for elementary or junior high students who have difficulty turning in assignments or completing homework at home. Some high schools have named such a study skill or tutoring group Academic Chances or Academic Opportunities.

Between Friends and Family: A group for family, sibling, or friendship concerns. Students of all ages seem to like this name.

Transitions: A group for students new to the school, returning from medical leave, experiencing changes in their lives due to the loss of a loved one, recovering from chemical use, and so on. Junior high and high school students like this name.

The Solution Seekers: A generic name for a generic group dealing with various issues, all of which seek refuge from the problem at hand.

Spreading the Word

Announcements about groups can be made at faculty meetings, Parent-Teacher Association meetings, and in the school newspaper. The names of contact persons are given to make the referral easier. Students should be able to self-refer themselves to a group. Since the groups meet before school, after school, during homeroom period, or during lunch period, there is little interference with school work, and teachers are cooperative. The group combines the resources of faculty, students, and educators. The entire process of developing, forming, and running the groups is done systemically and collaboratively.

Externalizing Problems in Groups

Epston and White (1990) talk of externalizing problems as a means of seeing them as intrusive in a person's life. This is an excellent approach for working with adolescents in groups, who developmentally may handle blame reluctantly, and children, who enjoy imaginative group processes and activities.

In the group setting, the idea of "removing the problem from your life" is a welcomed topic and applicable for groups dealing with study skill development or transitions or generic groups dealing with many different types of concerns.

Guiding Questions for Externalizing Problems in the Group Setting

The questions that follow, developed from the work of David Epston and Michael White, serve to guide and assist solution-focused school counselors in helping students free themselves of the problems that bother them:

1. What would your life be like without the problem? Who would be doing what?
2. How have you allowed the problem to interfere in your life?

3. What is it like when the problem is not affecting you as much? What are you doing during those times?

4. If you could visualize the problem, what would it look like?

5. How does the problem trick you into doing things you dislike later?

6. There must be times when the problem doesn't stand a chance, although it tries to bother you. How do you stop it?

7. If you could write a story or play and title it Chapter Two, omitting the problem, what would be different from your current Chapter One? Who would be in it?

8. From your description of the Chapter Two story or play, what are some things you could gradually do now to avoid the problem?

9. What would the audience applaud you doing when they watch you in Chapter Two?

10. Did anyone in the group see [group member]'s problem bother him or her in group today? [To the member:] How did you do that?

Externalizing with Elementary Students

Jean Cadell, a school counselor in Fort Worth, Texas, adopted the idea of externalizing and used it in small groups that dealt with anger. She held out her hands in a way that indicated larger or smaller to a group of six eight-year-old boys and asked them:

1. How big was your anger the last time it really bothered you?

2. How big is it now?

3. What have you done to shrink it?

4. How big do you want it to be today?

5. How will you do that?

At the end of a school day, one of her group members came up to her in the hall and said, "Ms. Cadell, help! I've got my anger back. Can I blow it into this paper bag and leave it in your office until tomorrow?" "Sure," she said, laughing. "Why not leave it here permanently?" He blew the "anger" into the bag, and left her office merrily.

Jean also began to ask the group members to draw their problem as a way of visually externalizing the problem. Her directions were, "Use your imagination, and pretend your problem is not you but something that bugs you sometimes. Use the crayons and paper, and draw what you think it might look like." She then asked them to think about how they would answer the following questions and put their answers on a chalkboard in two lists:

- How the problem bothers me: What it makes me do
- How I beat the problem: What I do to win

What My Problem Makes Me Do	How I Win Over the Problem
I argue with my teacher.	I put a QUIET note on my desk.
I get out of my seat.	I sit by myself.
I forget to raise my hand.	I remember my reward.

Jean then drew a scale on her wall, using the numbers 1 to 10, with 1 meaning "the problem is in control" and 10, "I am in control." After some discussion of how the problem made the students do poorly and how they could win or defeat the problem, she asked them to cut out the pictures. Without putting names on the drawings for confidentiality reasons, she asked the students to tape the pictures on the scale where they currently saw themselves in relation to the problem. Then each week she asked these questions:

"Based on what you have noticed and your teacher has noticed about you this week, where would you put your picture on the scale?"

"What would your teacher [or parent] say you did this week that meant you were in control?"

"How have you managed to move up? [or] How have you managed to stay the same or not move backward?"

"Where do you want to be when you come back to group next week?"

"Based on what you've told us today, how will you do this?"

"Do you all think your group members are where they should be on the scale?"

"Who do you think has done the best this week in defeating his or her problem?"

"What did you see him or her doing that tells you he or she, and not the problem, is in control?"

Generic Process Groups as Interventions

After Judy's parents divorced, her father felt that his daughter's interest in school and friends had changed. Judy, age sixteen, told her dad that she felt alone and sad most of the time. Judy and her mother had been close, and when her mother moved away, she felt abandoned. Her father called the school counselor and expressed his concerns about his daughter. The school counselor described a group he was forming specifically for students dealing with family concerns. The group was a generic group, which the students would name themselves, and was facilitated by the school counselor. Judy was reluctant to visit the group initially, so the counselor visited with her and talked with her about how she had dealt with other changes in her life before.

Judy said that in the past, she often talked to her best friend or her dad. She said her dad was pretty upset about the divorce, and she didn't want to burden him any more than she should with her sadness. She was ashamed and embarrassed that her mother had moved away and was living with a boyfriend. She often wondered if there could have been something she could have done differently to keep her mom from leaving. The counselor complimented her on her sensitivity to her dad's feelings and then asked her how she would like things to be for herself now that her parents were divorced. She said she wanted to be happy again, because things had been difficult for some time. The counselor asked Judy, "What will I see you doing some day very soon that will tell me you are slightly happier than today?"

Judy sat up in her chair, smiled a bit, and said she wanted to feel like being around others again. The counselor continued to build on Judy's ability to talk with him about her concerns, respect her dad's need for privacy, and talk with a best friend and her dad when she felt sad. Together the counselor and Judy decided to come up with a plan based on how Judy had handled situations of change in the past and how she now wanted things to be. When dealing with her sadness was described in this way, Judy agreed to try the group at least once, the same way she often tried other new situations.

The generic group met the following Tuesday morning before class. The group members were referred by teachers or parents or were self-referred. The school counselor wanted the group to be constructed in an interesting, helpful, and nonconfrontational manner. He discussed his role with the group the first day and described their time together as a way to talk about their concerns, learn about how they had solved problems in the past, and then leave with a plan to feel better. He assisted the group with a few basics: time, place, and compliments on times he heard the group members do well. He found that the group members made up their own rules quite effectively when he suggested how other groups had been run before. He began the first group with a request and a question: "I'm interested in all of you. Could you each please tell us briefly your reason for being in our group." And then: "How will you know when things are better for you?"

The counselor gave each student a file folder in which they made their own "case notes" each week. He asked the group for their comments and compliments on their peers' competencies often. Thereafter, the group basically ran itself, the counselor simply asking, "What's better this week?" at the beginning of each session. He marveled how quickly the students began asking each other this same question before he had a chance. This type of group usually ran for about six weeks. Within two weeks, Judy began associating with the members outside group time, became more expressive at home, and participated more in school activities. At the conclusion of the group, the counselor asked the members what had worked during the group time, and Judy told him that the process made her aware that her feelings were normal and that she no longer felt that her problems were as big as they had been.

Groups That Heal

Students who come for help with traumatic situations such as sexual, physical, or emotional abuse often view themselves as victims. However, many people who have experienced abuse are successful in careers, rear healthy children, and have rewarding lives. After clarifying that the abuse is no longer taking place by reporting it to proper authorities, students may approach this group as a way of defeating the influence of what has occurred. Phrases such as "escape from the problem" or "run from the problem" indicate that there is a way out. There is peace in knowing that one can run "from pain toward gain."

The group questions that follow are designed to focus on the abilities of students who have coped with such experiences so their lives may begin to be freed of the influence of the events rather than on past traumas. If a group member feels a need to describe the incident, time should be allowed. However, if the student seems to monopolize the group process with sad and upsetting descriptions, it is helpful for the counselor to inquire, "How is it helpful to you to share these stories with us?"

Following are suggested questions for a variety of groups that heal:

Ideas for Helping Group Members Through Trauma
1. Tell us briefly what you think we need to know about the reason you are each here today.
2. Describe times in your life when you have not allowed the situation to take control and keep you from enjoying life.
3. What's different when you are in control of the situation and you are doing what you want?

4. Someday soon when you are no longer troubled and imprisoned by this situation, how will your relationships improve?

5. On a scale of 1 to 10, with 1 being impossible and 10 being totally successful, where do you see yourself at this time in controlling the effects of your [sexual] issue on your relationships and your life?

6. Where would you like to be in the near future?

7. What can you each begin to do to increase your score?

8. What do some of you think others in this group can do to increase their score?

These questions can be discussed in each succeeding week:

"What has gone better for you?"

"Where are you on the scale?"

"How were you able to do that?"

Ideas for Groups Dealing with Family Issues

1. If a miracle happened tonight when you were asleep and tomorrow you awoke to find things much better with your friend or family, how would things be different?

2. Tell us a time when that happened, even slightly.

3. What were you doing to help that happen? What specifically would we have seen you do that worked better for you and your friend or family?

4. How did you do that?

5. How can you do that again now?

6. When things get better for you and your friend or family, what will you get to do more of?

7. On a scale of 1 to 10, with 10 being totally successful in accomplishing what you say you want with your friend and family and 1 being totally unsuccessful, where were you when you came to group today? Where are you now?

8. Where would you like to be by the time the group meets again?

9. How will you do that, just for a few days [one week]?

10. I'd like the group members to watch [group member's name] this week and notice when you see him or her more at ease and less bothered by this problem.

Ideas for Groups Dealing with Substance Abuse

1. How has drinking/using drugs kept you from succeeding in your life and living the way you want to live?

2. What will you get to do when alcohol/drugs are no longer a concern for you and others in your life?

3. Who will probably notice first that you are in control?

4. What have you tried in the past to control your drinking/drugs? List and then cross out unsuccessful strategies while asking, "Did it work?" Recognize that the unmarked strategies are strategies that work.

5. When did you last find yourself in control of the problem with alcohol/drugs? How were you able to do this? Where were you? Who was there, or not there?

6. On a scale of 1 to 10, with 1 being completely taken over by alcohol/drugs and 10 being in control of alcohol/drugs, where would you like to be when we meet again?

7. Based on the exceptions that you told us today, how will you do that?

Keeping Track of Group Members

Keep track of group members and their achievements weekly, and you will have ample exceptions for compliments and writing notes. See the sample below. On the lines, list the member's name and then the competency or exception that developed during the group time. Consider a short note to the group member who truly amazed you!

Name   **Exception/Competency**

1. _____

_____

2. _____

_____

3. _____

_____

4. _____

_____

5. _____

_____

6. _____

_____

7. _____

_____

Parent Groups

While working with a group of graduate students, Anita McNew learned about the solution-focused approach and took it home to use with her eight-year-old daughter, Monica. When she reported her successes the following week, her excitement was contagious, encouraging other graduate students who were parents to try the approach. She contributed the following summary of what she did, how it affected her relationship with her daughter, and how the intervention changed her home atmosphere completely:

I have a bright, loving, eight-year-old daughter named Monica. As a toddler, Monica was a joy. She was easy-going, compliant, and eager to please. Yet lately, things had not been going well. One ongoing issue involved her getting ready to leave in the morning in a timely fashion. The mornings usually deteriorated into yelling and crying as we tried to get out of the house on time.

I have been a working mother since Monica was three years old. During all of that time, I could count on one hand the times we actually left the house on time. I was chronically late for work, both of my daughters were tardy for school, and all of us were late for church. It was very frustrating. I have read every parenting article I could find, and I've listened to everyone's suggestions. I thought I had tried everything: rewarding, bargaining, bribing, taking away privileges, reasoning, yelling, crying, you name it! Nothing was effective.

After hearing about the solution-focused approach for just one day, I decided to try out the few techniques that were discussed. I figured I had nothing to lose. It sounded too easy, and I was skeptical, but thought that it was worth a try.

On the way home from church one evening (for which we were late, of course), I started talking to Monica about the events of the morning. I had to work very hard at not using terms like *problem, wrong,* and *bad.* That was challenging and different from the language I had learned from my parents. I started the conversation by telling Monica how impressed I was that she could accomplish so much every week at her young age. I told her I was amazed at the way she goes to dance twice a week, finishes all of her homework ahead of time, reads nearly every night, bathes herself, gets herself ready for school and church, and helps feed the dog and cats. She seemed very pleased with these remarks, smiling broadly.

Then I mentioned that it seemed funny to me that such an amazing kid had such a hard time getting ready on time in the mornings. I asked her what she thought it would be like if she could get up in the morning in a pleasant mood and get ready on time. She stated that she would not feel so rushed, I would not be yelling, she would not be crying, she would not get a tardy mark at school, I would not be late for work or lose my job, and she might even have time to watch a little TV before school. I told her that I really didn't like yelling at her or making her cry, and that I appreciated that she cared about whether I was late for work. I said that it all sounded like a great way to start the day to me. She agreed.

I then told her that I was having a hard time understanding why someone like her would have such a tough time in the mornings and asked her if she had any idea about why that was the case. She said, "I just can't get up as quickly as you do in the morning. It takes my eyes a while to open." I asked her if she had any ideas about how to help her wake up in the morning. She suggested that I come into her room thirty minutes before she had to be up, turn on the radio, turn on her closet light, open the closet door wide enough to let some light into the room, and come back later. This was curious to me, because my husband had tried this in the past, to no avail. But I kept my impulsive parent mouth shut and complimented her brilliance for coming up with such a great idea. We went on to talk about how the next morning would look when we did these things.

The very next morning, we tried it. It worked. She was up when she needed to be, was in a pleasant mood, and was ready with time to spare. I couldn't compliment her enough. The compliments weren't some parenting technique either; they were absolutely sincere. I couldn't believe it. Of course, my optimism about the future mornings was guarded. Surely it couldn't be this simple. Well, it has been over three weeks, and we have not been late leaving the house one time. Not one time! Not only that, but Monica has been generally more pleasant and compliant all around. When asked to do something, she doesn't roll her eyes, groan, or stomp her feet quite as often. It's like having the old Monica back.

My next challenge will be to approach my other daughters with a more positive, affirming attitude. I can certainly see now how tackling a "problem" by identifying exceptions is more effective than by blaming. Then I would like to help my husband adopt some of these techniques. Perhaps I'll use solution-focused techniques on him!

Solution-focused parenting groups are times when parents can come together and learn from each other. Too often parenting groups have a curriculum that teaches new parenting skills that experts have developed. Certainly many of these programs are invaluable, particularly to new parents, but seasoned parents often look for solutions to problems that are already occurring.

Parenting groups can follow the same format explained previously in this chapter. What will be different is the effort that it might take to keep parents from complaining about their child and their child's problems. However, when this happens, the focus changes from changing the child or adolescent to examining parenting skills that work and do not work. Within these powerful conversations, change can happen.

Group Meetings After the First One

The next group meeting begins with a familiar tone, using the same format as in beginning a solution-focused group process. If a student does not have many improvements to report and prefers to talk about what did not work, the following statements may help him to get back on a solution track: "Tell us about your worst day. Now tell us a day when it was slightly better than that." Then follow up: "Let's suppose that more of that happens. What do you want to happen for you by the time we see you again?" and then, "In spite of things being rough, you still came back to group. What do you all think that says about you?"

The group then takes on a life of its own, talking about what went better the previous week, relating those changes to the goals that were addressed during the first session, and then talking about what the next steps will be.

When, Where, and How to Start

Initially in most schools, a group forms from the suggestions of teachers or parents regarding the kinds of groups needed and the times for groups to meet at school. Parents are sent information on counseling services and encouraged to call and suggest their ideas for groups. Soliciting ideas seems to lessen questions about what is going on in school, gives parents opportunities to provide their ideas, and makes school more collaborative. The Teacher Suggestions for Group Counseling handout can be given to teachers and administrators. This handout requests educator participation for two reasons:

- Educators experience the needs of their students daily in the classroom. Their thoughts are a valuable resource in determining the kinds of groups that would be helpful.

- When educators are asked for their ideas, they become part of the process and decision making. This lessens their resistance when students leave class for group.

Assuring educators that the counseling groups will not interfere with their daily instruction is also important in creating cooperation.

Teacher Suggestions for Group Counseling

Dear Teacher,

The counseling department is interested in your ideas regarding group counseling for our students. These groups will not interfere with your class time and will meet before school, during lunch, or after school. It is my hope that these groups will assist in our discovery of competencies in students to solve their own concerns. On the lines below, please list various concerns or issues you might be aware of with your students. Please return this to me by: _____

Thanks!

School Counselor

SUGGESTIONS

Example: A group for students who display inappropriate anger

_____

_____

_____

_____

_____

_____

_____

_____

_____

_____

_____

Parental Consent

Most school districts require parental permission for a student to participate in group counseling, especially in the primary grades. Once again, cooperation lessens resistance. This opportunity for inquiry alerts parents that the school is on the side of the student and is considering the student's welfare. The legal requirements are also met with a signed permission form (see the Parent Consent for Group Counseling form).

Parent Consent for Group Counseling

Dear Parent or Guardian,

Your son/daughter, _____

has an opportunity to attend the _____
group at our school. The time for this group will be:

_____ on _____ [day]. The group will not
conflict with class instruction.

It is my plan to assist the students in this confidential group with identifying
their strengths and abilities to solve their own concerns. The group will meet for

_____ weeks, unless your son/daughter decides to stop attending. Your
permission for your son/daughter will be appreciated. Please feel free to call the
school with any questions.

Please return by: _____

Thanks!

_____, School Counselor

.... detach here ....

PARENT PERMISSION

_____ has my permission

to attend group counseling at _____ (school),

during the _____ (year) school year.

_____
Parent/Guardian Signature

When to Begin Solution-Focused Groups

The second month of the school year or semester or quarter seems to be the best time to solicit group ideas from teachers. Giving teachers an initial period in school to observe students and deal with other required documentation and planning is considerate and beneficial. They will appreciate your consideration. Group counseling, after all, is designed to accommodate students and educators. The right time, the right group, and cooperation make for a good group counseling program.

Pitfalls and Safeguards: Let the Group Do the Work

Solution-focused groups offer a refreshing opportunity to join with others who have similar dilemmas and learn from each other about times when problems are not as pervasive in their lives. The exceptions that are identified by several members become strategies to consider and identify with, opening the door again to times when problems do not happen as often. A parent who recognizes that talking with her son while driving to school is more pleasant than talking at home at ten o'clock at night when the son is tired has learned a new strategy. When a parent recognizes that the ten-year-old who balks at her bath by having a tantrum, yet finishes the tantrum after five minutes, she learns to say, "Susie, I know you will have the tantrum before your bath, so go ahead." Then Susie stops the tantrum. When the father, an attorney, uses his negotiating skills with his fifteen-year-old son about his grades and curfew, refusing to yell or criticize, the son is compliant. These ideas, when discussed and even written down by the group counselor, can become new maps to follow on the road to parental satisfaction. Learn to listen for exceptions during group, and those members who can't seem to identify them on their own will become competent before your eyes.

Action Plan: Listen to the School Staff

At your next faculty meeting, ask teachers and staff to describe their concerns about students. From that information, form several groups that meet weekly that you think would begin to meet the needs of the students. In elementary school, look for curriculum that is strengths based and incorporate solution-focused ideas into the curriculum. Consider placing scaling numbers on your office wall or wherever else your group meets and asking students each week to scale where they are in reference to the group issue.

For secondary students, keep the group process oriented, without the curriculum, since these students are ready to talk about themselves and need time to process where they are going and how they might get there using exceptions. Write them notes afterward if you have time, mentioning what you noticed them doing differently during group. Then as the group ends, consider presenting certificates that you and the students compose together during the group. These can be invaluable to remind the students of how they accomplished their goals. Parents can also be sent letters commending them on having an ambitious student, with student permission.

Send out permission letters for students in the elementary grades to inform parents of the group process. Secondary students may not need letters of consent. Check with your school administrator for guidance.

Chapter Six

The Solution-Focused School

*If a teacher is indeed wise he does not bid you enter
the house of his wisdom, but rather leads you to the
threshold of your own mind.*

—Kahlil Gibran

One might think that in order to start a solution-focused school program, the school must be of a certain caliber and have certain types of programs that the school program can be adapted to. That is not necessarily so. All it takes is a vision and a desire to do things differently. Take note of the following innovative alternative school that deals with some of the most challenging and at-risk students of a large school district.

The Little High School That Did

Garza Independence High School is an alternative school in Austin, Texas, where its school family uses the solution-focused approach in every aspect of its operation. When the training occurred, the teachers, administrators, school counselors, teacher aides, and janitors attended. This effort to encompass the support and context of the entire school staff made the atmosphere that of support, competence, and respect.

The school, in existence since 1999, was designed for eleventh and twelfth graders who seek an alternative way to complete high school studies. Garza has between 350 and 400 students. It adopted a solution-building philosophy from solution-focused therapy when the high school was conceived, and the school administrators and staff adopted the process and techniques of solution-focused therapy to match the school mission. Its goal was to create a strengths-oriented school whose culture and philosophy are consistent with the change process of the solution-focused model.

According to Franklin and Streeter (2003, p. 11), eight characteristics enable Garza High School to be considered a solution-building school:

1. Faculty emphasis on building strengths of students
2. Attention given to individual relationships and progress of the students
3. Emphasis upon student choices and personal responsibility
4. Overall commitment to achievement and hard work
5. Trust in student evaluations
6. Focus on student's future success instead of past difficulties
7. Celebrating small steps toward success
8. Reliance on goal-setting activities

The administrators at Garza High School developed a mission statement that is both relational and individualized to reflect the major values and philosophy of the solution-building school: "Gonzalo Garza Independence High School shall foster a community of empowered learners in an atmosphere of mutual respect and trust where every individual is challenged to learn, grow, and accomplish goals now and in the future" (Franklin & Streeter, 2003, p. 13).

All individuals—administrators, facilitators (teachers), staff, and students—are expected to practice and model the Garza Code of Honor:

- Demonstrate personal honor and integrity at all times.
- Choose peace over conflict.
- Respect for ourselves and others [Franklin & Streeter, 2003, p. 13].

Exhibit 6.1 provides a list of statements reflecting the students' enforcement of the code of honor. Each student is given this code of honor and is expected to follow it. The staff reinforce the code by their own behaviors, similar to the code.

Exhibit 6.1: Statements Reflecting Students' Enforcement of the Code of Honor

- Students are not given suspension, but "reflection" when they do something wrong.

- Students are loyal to the school and protective of other students and the school environment.

- Students become more independent and confident because they take personal responsibility for their success.

- The students trust staff.

- Students need more self-discipline to succeed at Garza because they are given a lot of freedom.

- Students do not have fights.

- Students are mature.

- Students respect the campus and code of honor.

- Teachers treat students with respect.

- Students treat teachers with respect.

- Students respect each other.

- Students get to know teachers, counselors, administrators, and staff on an individual basis.

- During disciplinary situations there is also evidence that students take personal responsibility for breaking the code of honor.

Source: Franklin & Streeter (2003, p. 14).

Better Relationships, Better Results

Franklin and Streeter (2003) write:

Research indicates that positive student-teacher interactions and increased support from teachers are associated with higher academic achievement. . . . Adolescents view teachers who treat students as individuals and who demonstrate a desire to know students on a personal level as more caring, which can increase student's motivation. . . . Students who have more positive student/teacher interactions and feel that their teachers care about them also tend to like school more. . . . A close student-teacher relationship can be especially important with at-risk children who may have experienced repeated school failure and poor relationships with teachers. . . . Students with weak bonds to teachers and school are more likely to have a low GPA, which is in turn a risk factor for substance use and ultimately dropout [p. 18].

Franklin and Streeter (2003) mentioned that many students interviewed at Garza High School cited not liking their previous school, and particularly not liking teachers or administrators, as a reason for changing schools:

Sixty-five percent of the students mentioned that their relationship with the teachers was the primary difference between Garza and their prior high school. Moreover, it became evident while reading through the transcribed interviews that the students' close relationships with their teachers helped remove several of their barriers to academic success. The students mentioned a wide range of examples of how important their relationship with their teachers was. Ivan and Jennifer provided two extreme examples of teachers going beyond the call of duty to help them in times of need. Ivan, who was incarcerated for ten days because of a drug possession charge, explains how his close relationship with the teachers helped him through this hardship:

"For a quick example, I was incarcerated. All these teachers, they came for me. They had my work ready. One of my teachers even drove to the juvenile hall to give me my homework. What kind of school would do that for its students? Most schools would just look at you and say, 'Obviously you haven't learned your lesson. You're not the kind of students that we need here.' But here they say, 'We still see good in this kid. He may have done bad things but haven't we all.' And when I came back, every teacher gave me a hug."

Jennifer was also a beneficiary of teachers going beyond their call of duty. Jennifer was home while she was in the final weeks of her pregnancy, not able to attend school. Jennifer stated, "On Homebound, that's what you go on when you are pregnant, they bring the work to you, over there [at her old traditional public school] they had a teacher but over here they actually bring the work to you."

Both students recognize these events as core differences between teachers at Garza High School and teachers from their traditional high school. The teachers seemed to enable the students to feel a sense of uniqueness, which made them desire success academically in that teacher's class, both educationally and behaviorally [pp. 80–81].

More Possibilities Than Problems

The solution-focused school program offers more possibilities than the problem-focused school because its focus on strengths and abilities literally resurrects self-esteem and competence in students and teachers. The approach is particularly helpful with students who seem to pass through the discipline office in a revolving door because the current discipline plan fails to work. And in many schools, when students do not fit neatly into the "box" designated by school officials, they become unmotivated academically and feel lost. That is why every student who stays and graduates from Garza High School goes on to college. Instead of casting these students into lower classifications and disciplinary actions over and over again, the solution-focused approach at Garza teaches students that given a context in which they can be competent, they can and will be successful.

Using a solution-focused framework, Garza Independence High School has also integrated many of the effective practices in education for alternative schools, dropout prevention, and retrieval strategies.

Integrate Solution-Focused Ideas into Your School . . . Now!

In today's busy classrooms, weaknesses and struggles become the focus as teachers try to create environments for learning in surroundings that are often quite negative and problem focused. And as teachers try to keep classroom order, strengths of students can go unnoticed. It seems difficult to decide who suffers the most: the students, unnoticed for their strengths due to their misbehavior, or the teachers, burned out from being disciplinarians with little energy left for creative teaching. Caught in a difficult situation, many teachers respond negatively toward their students. The students in turn respond defensively, and learning becomes a scarce commodity.

Past theories of educational discipline techniques and behavior modification approaches waited for students to prove to educators that they knew how to act in school. However, today's schools now have stresses of peer pressure coupled with falling parental involvement. One has to wonder if we have created such an environment that keeps parents away. Maybe it's time to do more than place stars on good papers. Maybe it's time to notice when students pass or come near passing and ask them, "How did you do that?" Educators who have used solution-focused ideas in volatile schools report that the students who once flinched when the teacher touched their paper now look to the teacher as nurturing. Let's see how a solution-focused approach can change things.

Getting Started with the Student: The Teacher Referral Form

The Teacher Referral Form was designed to put the responsibility of dealing with teacher-student conflict in the hands of the teacher and student involved. The form itself came about from the comments of educators who began to list exceptions instead of problems on paper when visiting with students. Many educators often found themselves overwhelmed with such referrals. While individual work can be successful, counselors and administrators do not have the time to conduct in-depth sessions. Furthermore, most problems can be solved more quickly if the system (teacher, parent, peers, counselor, classmates) is included in the process. Most educators who have begun using solution-focused ideas have found their students to be less resistant as they avidly write down the student's exceptions. The educators also found that  many parents began to cooperate more when they saw the Teacher Referral Form and perceived that the school was more interested in growth and competency building than in punitive actions.

Teacher Referral Form

Dear Teacher,

Thank you for your referral of _____. I am arranging a meeting with the student and his or her parents if that is appropriate. Below, please list the times when you notice _____ doing WELL in class. These observations will be very helpful to this student and me as we talk about some solutions to the concerns you have.

Please be as specific as possible—for example, "Olivia did well in class today when she chose to sit by herself while completing her assignment."

1. _____

_____

2. _____

_____

3. _____

_____

4. _____

_____

5. _____

_____

Thanks.

_____
Teacher Signature

I have used this form with elementary and high school students. Surprisingly, high school teachers were especially appreciative of the idea, since it has a different kind of request: positive comments for their students. Students are always curious about what teachers think about them. Administrators have also used the form as a positive reinforcement for students who were in their offices too frequently. Noticing the student in the hall, behaving in the lunchroom, or receiving no referrals from the teacher for a week are all reasons to write a small note or send the form to a student during homeroom class. It takes little time to jot down a few comments; the results, according to those who have sent such notes, can last much longer.

This form works well in parent conferences by promoting teacher cooperation and student interest. School counselors who choose to use the form should obtain an administrative signature at the top of the sheet before the student passes the forms out to his or her teacher. Teachers are busy people, and one more form often seems monumental. Assistance from the appropriate hierarchical level will probably ensure more cooperation from a busy teacher in completing the form. The form can also take the place of weekly progress reports, which many concerned parents request that their children solicit from teachers. Building goodwill between home and school is accomplished when parents receive a form describing behaviors that teachers deem successful or competent. The form can be used in the form of weekly or biweekly information for a few weeks or an entire term. Eventually the students may decide to listen for exceptions themselves or be told by the teachers what is working.

Working with Referred Students

The assessment session after a referral is made is itself an intervention. The student who talks with the counselor and hears the exceptions written down by his teacher should learn three things.

First, the school is on the student's side; the educators are here to assist him or her in being successful, not point out what is wrong. Alignment with students is very important. This does not mean that the student is viewed as innocent; rather, he or she is considered to be in need of assistance from school staff to understand his or her competency. When schools approach children and adolescents with confrontation and as problems, the students often behave as such and respond rebelliously. When students are approached in a firm manner yet are asked to self-evaluate themselves for competencies, they are given the chance to prove that they can behave differently. When we cooperate with students', teachers', and parents' worldviews, we lessen resistance. Even the angriest student or teacher will calm down when he or she senses an empathetic educator. Resistance is lessened when both people are on the same side. Schools should be on the side of the student and not contribute to struggling interactions. An educator who says that the student was wise to come to the counselor and that there is a problem is aligning with the student. I like to think of the solution-focused method as a model in which I become a travel guide or consultant. I'm led by the student, teacher, or parent who shows me the way; I get to point out the scenery he or she misses while in distress.

Second, change can be attractive to the student. Students tend to blame others—it is, after all, much easier to consider someone else at fault for our failures. Aligning with students and then asking, "What will your teacher see you doing that will keep  him from sending you back to my office?" will encourage a student to make changes and cause others to change in response. Asking a student, "What do you think it will take for you to get

Mr. S off your back?" is a good way of aligning with the student and motivating this young person to receive some sort of relief. A student can also become more motivated when asked, "What will be better when Mr. S treats you better in class in response to your new ways of behaving?"

Third, the student is already competent. Students who progress one grade after another each year (even if they are held back once or twice) are successful in at least that way. The student who goes three days a week without being sent to the office is behaviorally competent three days a week. Pointing out these abilities to stay out of trouble three days a week builds competent feelings and reinforces the student's ability to do more of what works on those days. For a junior in high school, for example, a new geometry course may be presenting too many new challenges, and he or she may feel lost. Asking the student how he or she might have handled other new situations in the past may lead to ideas for solutions. Many of us have ways of handling situations that fall into categories: stress, anger, worry, frustration, new job, new relationships, too much to do, and so on. Helping students and teachers realize that they have already accomplished similar feats causes their anxiety to diminish.

Here is an example of a student assessment using the guiding questions:

COUNSELOR: Glad to see you today, Jake. Sorry it's under such rough circumstances, though. What would Mrs. Jones say her reason was for sending you here?

STUDENT: She says I'm lazy and uncooperative. I think she just doesn't like me. Besides, her class is a pain. I usually sleep through it, it's so boring.

COUNSELOR: Yeah, sometimes it is tough to stay awake. Gee, does it happen all the time that you forget to cooperate and sleep through class?

STUDENT: Oh, no. Sometimes I do my work—it just has to be interesting and I can't sit by my friends.

COUNSELOR: Oh, really. That's interesting. You know, I haven't seen you at all this year, and as I look at your record here, I notice that you've been passing all your other subjects. That's six out of seven classes.

STUDENT: Yeah. I've been passing.

COUNSELOR: How have you done that? I mean you've passed six classes out of seven!

STUDENT: My old man is on me and rewards me for it. Plus, I like the other teachers. I think they like me too.

COUNSELOR: What does that do for you, Jake, when you think the teacher likes you?

STUDENT: Makes me feel like working. I try to cooperate a little—you know, try and help them out. They help me out sometimes too when they know I need it.

COUNSELOR: So all you have to do is notice when the teacher is helpful toward you, do your work, and cooperate, as you say, and you pass the class?

STUDENT: Yeah, I guess.

COUNSELOR: Tell you what, Jake, see this form? [the Teacher Referral Form] When Mrs. Jones referred you to my office, I gave her this to fill out. If you look at it, you'll notice that it asks her to watch for times when she sees you do well in class.

STUDENT: Okay.

COUNSELOR: She's going to send it back to me tomorrow. Until then, what do you say about doing whatever you've been doing in the other classes so she can put down some of those times you do well? For just a couple of days. What do you say?

STUDENT: I guess so.

COUNSELOR: One more thing, Jake. Between now and when I see you again, watch for signs that Mrs. Jones likes you.

STUDENT: She doesn't.

COUNSELOR: Just watch, okay? You seem like a pretty observant guy. You know when other teachers like you and need your help.

STUDENT: That's true.

In this dialogue, the counselor stepped into the student's worldview by not blaming Jake or his teacher. Jake focused on the teacher having the problem, and the counselor focused on the other teachers in Jake's day who did not have a problem with him. By assisting Jake to realize that he did indeed have success in other classes, he was more prone to do more of what worked in other classes. On follow-up, the following questions can be asked:

"What's better?"

"If I were to have watched you during the past week [days, weeks], what do you think I would have seen you doing that was different from before?"

"Who else might have noticed you doing things differently?"

"What do you want to keep on doing that's working for you now?"

"On a scale of 1 to 10, if 1 means the problem is in charge and 10 you are in charge, where were you the first time you came here? Where are you now? How have you helped this to change?"

The Note That Made the Difference

Students who admit things are better may fear that such admissions are hazardous to relationships with counselors, administrators, and others. (They might like the attention!) Be persistent and let the students know that you will be glad to see them in a new and different context—and out of trouble. One way to keep up the new and important relationship between educator and student is through note writing. David Epston, a therapist from New Zealand and coauthor of *Narrative Means to Therapeutic Ends* (1990), routinely sends written notes after he meets with students, teachers, and parents. He summarizes the visit, notes his impressions, and adds compliments and tasks. This could be used for a student as follows:

Dear Latisha,

I enjoyed meeting with you today in my office. I was amazed at your ability to point out times when the problem did not bother you in your other classes. You said six out of seven classes went well. I was also impressed by your plan to move to the front of the room so you are not distracted, since that apparently works well in your algebra class. Good luck! Stop by to let me know how things go. I'm pulling for you.

Mrs. Smith, School Counselor

A similar note can be sent to Latisha's teacher:

Dear Mrs. Thomas,

Thanks for referring Latisha. She and I appreciated your comments on the referral sheet. She has since told me that moving to the front of the class has been helpful. Thanks for your cooperation during this busy season at school. You were wise to refer Latisha: she is a bright student! Please continue to notice the behavior that you see as effective and let her know. She has told me she likes the attention! Thanks!

Mrs. Smith, School Counselor

Information from Students: Our Clues to Success

The Student Information Sheet asks the student to communicate what would be helpful and can be even more effective when done collaboratively with an administrator or parent. The solution-focused school counselor phrases its purpose in this way: "You know, I truly believe that we just simply do not understand what you need from us here at Smith Junior High School. You have done well during the past six months, but obviously things are changing for you that we don't have information for. Today I'd like you to do an inventory for us, and watch as you go through your day for times when you do okay in class."

Student Information Sheet

Dear Student,

Your teachers and I are interested in assisting you here at school. Below, please list the times when you think you do better in school. (Think about the past few months or last year.) Please be specific. This is your chance to tell us what you think will help you do better more often. For example, "I do better in school when I think the teacher likes me; I understand the homework assignment; I place my assignment in my book to turn it in; when the teacher calls on me and does not ignore my answer."

1. _____

_____

2. _____

_____

3. _____

_____

4. _____

_____

5. _____

_____

What worked for me in class this week:

_____

_____

_____

_____
Student Signature

The probability is that students who pay attention to their behavior will change behaviors as well. Asking the student to talk to teachers about his or her needs will increase collaboration between teacher and student. A shy student may prefer placing the form in the teacher's box or give it to the teacher directly. The importance of this venture is to let the teacher know that the student is attempting to change. With high school students, this form may not be necessary, but the idea is still helpful. A conference with a high school teacher might offer the student an opportunity to say what he or she needs from the teacher. Preparing the teacher about how the student will approach the conference might be valuable. Often, one on one with teachers is difficult for students. The teacher could be informed that the student wants to try a different approach to working things out: instead of talking about the problem, he or she wants to discuss what might be helpful to his or her learning, behaving, or participating in class.

In addition, this exercise teaches students to look at themselves differently, as if they are able to accomplish tasks. The student has a better chance to become the expert on himself or herself and is more likely to ask a personal question such as, "What works for me?" the next time a problem crops up. If we as educators can assist students with this practical way of perceiving and dealing with everyday situations, we have truly given them a gift for a less stressful life.

The Solution-Focused Parent Conference

The parent-conference role play included in this section shows how the Student Information Sheet and the Teacher Referral Form can be used together to arrive at solutions with parents that are important to all involved. It represents the efforts of all concerned and creates the atmosphere of responsibility on the part of everyone to stop maintaining what is perceived to be a problem.

For many parents, a conference entails hearing about how bad things are at school, and many parents consider themselves failures or feel that the school has failed their child. Instead, a solution-focused approach can rescue the school, teachers, and administrators from being blamed. The dialogue spreads the responsibility throughout; everyone's ideas are solicited and considered before the strategy is developed. The Guide Sheet for Parent Conferences is provided.

The following statements and questions are suggestions that might be useful in making parent conferences more pleasant and empowering to both student and parent:

1. *Information gathering—parent empowerment:* "Mrs. Johnson, I want you to know how impressed I am that you came to our meeting so willingly. Obviously you know that Darryl needs your assistance. Can you tell me exactly what you're seeing at home or at school regarding Darryl that concerns you? . . . You know, that's really in agreement with what we're seeing in him here at school."

2. *Searching for exceptions:* "Mrs. Johnson, I'm really curious about the times when you do not see Darryl experiencing troubles with his schoolwork. Can you tell me about those times? . . . Which days, how many hours a week, or how many times a week do you notice Darryl not experiencing troubles? . . . So, when Darryl is [on a schedule, when you're right there with

him, when you check his work, when he is not fighting with siblings, when his homework is done on time, when he thinks the teacher likes him] school is a little easier. Is that correct?"

3. *Changing problem thinking to solution thinking:* "That's really interesting, Mrs. Johnson, because when I asked the teacher who referred Darryl to me to fill out the sheets I have here [Teacher Referral Form], I found there were similar times to what you're describing, plus other times when Darryl did better. These sheets list the times here at school when he does better in class. We're interested in those times here because we really want him to succeed. . . . I have one more sheet to share with you, Mrs. Johnson. It's a sheet that Darryl filled out for us. On this sheet are his views about when school goes better for him. He said that he does better in class when [the student feels the teacher likes him, is not as tired, is not sitting in the back of the room, is not worried about you and his dad, spends time with you, and does not have to baby-sit during weeknights]."

4. *Developing tasks for solutions:* "Mrs. Johnson, based on what Darryl has told us works for him, what his teachers have said works better, and what you have said works, what would you suggest we try with him for a few days this week?"

5. *Suggesting success:* "Mrs. Johnson, I appreciate your time today. Your suggestions really make sense. I guess I'd like to ask you one more quick question: When Darryl does better more often in school and you see that happening, what will you and he get to do more of that you aren't doing now?"

As the language suggests, the school, parent, and student agree that success lies in the solutions noticed by all involved. Notice the language used in the dialogue: "When [student name] does better" and "What will you get to do when [student name] does better?" This suggestion that things will improve encourages hope. Parents whose children are in trouble at school often come to school concerned, feeling like failures themselves. By offering suggestions of the teachers, students, and parents themselves, there is virtually no threat of failure. I tend to mention in training sessions that I never ask anyone to do anything that they have never done before. There is no risk of failure that way. Instead, I may suggest they do more of what worked in other situations. For example, a mom who worries about her sixteen-year-old daughter's association with friends she does not know can observe how she has set limits with her driving last summer. The daughter always told her where she was going and with whom when she drove the car, or she lost the privilege for a day. By applying the same ideas for friends by requiring her daughter to introduce them and leave a phone number or address as to her destination (or she loses a night out), the mom may worry less and feel more comfortable.

Guide Sheet for Parent Conferences

1. Information gathering: Getting everyone's concern.

Parent's view:

_____

_____

_____

_____

School's view:

_____

_____

_____

_____

2. Searching for exceptions: Times when the concern happens less.

Can you tell me when the problem doesn't bother your son/daughter?

Parent's view:

_____

_____

_____

_____

School's view:

_____

_____

_____

_____

Guide Sheet for Parent Conferences (cont.)

3. Presentation of exceptions collected from teachers

Summary of exceptions: Give Teacher Information Forms and the Student Information Sheet to the parent.

_____

_____

_____

_____

_____

4. Task development: Choosing strategies to be implemented only from the identified exceptions.

Parent:

_____

_____

_____

School staff:

_____

_____

_____

The Solution-Focused Individualized Education Plan

Developing solution-focused educational plans for special education students already in programs uses identifying exceptions to the pathological behavior. The Individualized Education Plan (IEP) described here enlists the help of all teachers associated with the student, especially teachers whose classes the student is passing. The IEP can be accompanied by test scores and other forms relative to the special education program in individual states. The ideas noted in the IEP focus on the student's abilities and competencies and the identification of such abilities. The solution-focused ideas, noted with an asterisk in the worksheet, encourage creativity. Use of the Teacher Referral Form for the identification of effective teaching methods is helpful.

The development of the IEP presented here grew from my personal experience with what Texas educators refer to as ARD meetings: meetings for admission, review, and dismissal, usually held for special education students to determine treatment options. When my youngest son's short attention span was affecting his learning and efficiency in class, his teachers and I wanted to do something different for him. After sitting through the ARD with his vice principal, speech therapist, and three of his teachers, I wondered, "Where do we go now?"

We had spoken only about the problems, not solutions. I asked the two teachers what they thought they did that helped him remember to turn in his assignments and bring home his homework. As they described what they thought they did, his third teacher acknowledged that she might try their tactics as well. I felt fortunate to have worked with such a receptive staff. The ideas were accepted readily and implemented. He began to do much better in class.

Individualized Education Plan

Name: _____ Grade: _____

A. Competencies:

1. Physical, as it affects participation in instructional settings:

    ❏ No physical limitations, no modification of regular class needed

    ❏ Some physical limitations, no modification of regular class needed

    ❏ Needs modifications because of the following impairment:

_____

_____

*In what activities does the impairment not affect the student? List specific activities:

_____

_____

*Describe modifications needed, based on the above activities:

_____

_____

2. Physical, as it affects physical education:

The student is capable of receiving instruction in the essential elements of physical education through the regular program without modifications:

    ❏ Yes

    ❏ No

*If NO, list the following activities in which the student has shown capabilities of receiving instruction:

_____

_____

Individualized Education Plan (cont.)

*Recommendation, based on competency in listed activities in number 2:

_____

_____

B. Behavioral:

1. Educational placement and programming:

❑ No modifications

❑ Has some characteristics that may affect learning, although not severe enough to withdraw from regular classes: _____ poor task completion: _____ impulsive—requires reminding to work slowly.

❑ Distractible—may require isolation, sit at front of room, and so on at times: _____ other: _____

❑ *Abilities that emerge in specific learning tasks and activities and enhance cooperation in the classroom, as identified by teachers, administrators, and parents:

_____

_____

_____

2. Ability to follow disciplinary rules:

❑ _____ Appropriate for age and cultural group. May be treated the same as nonhandicapped student. Student should be able to follow the district's discipline management plan. Student is responsible for school board rules and campus policies without modifications.

❑ _____ *This student is responsible for school board rules and campus procedure. A modified discipline plan will be used. The following approaches have been identified as effective in working with this student through direct observation by teachers, administrators, and parents:

_____

_____

_____

Individualized Education Plan (cont.)

C. Prevocational/Vocational (when appropriate): Skills that may be prerequisite to vocational education. Rate using the following scale: 1 to 10, where 1 = completely unskilled and 10 = completely competent:

_____ cognitive skills	_____ expressive skills
_____ reading level	_____ organizational skills
_____ performance	_____ social skills
_____ verbal comprehension	_____ following directions
_____ attendance	_____ personal hygiene/self-care
_____ punctuality	
_____ other _____	

*Using all skills with a rating of 6 or above, list opportunities within the school program that seem appropriate for the listed competencies:

_____

_____

_____

_____

_____

D. Academic/Developmental: (Grade or age levels alone are not sufficient.)

1. Indicate the content areas in which the student is competent and can receive instruction in the regular or remedial program without modification:

❏ all subjects	❏ reading	❏ math	❏ social studies
❏ English	❏ science	❏ spelling	❏ computer literacy
❏ health	❏ vocational	❏ fine arts	❏ physical education
❏ other _____			

Individualized Education Plan (cont.)

2. *Based on the identified subject competencies and collaboration with the assigned teacher, list the identified subject below and a brief explanation of the teaching methods identified as effective with this student. Examples are individual work, group work, isolation from peers = less distractibility, individual library assignments/ projects, visual stimulation, seating arranged near the teacher, parent cooperation/ collaboration, journal, rewards, and dates assigned to assignments.

Subject   **Effective Teaching Methods**

3. Indicate the content areas in which the student's competency development needs assistance from a special education program:

❑ all subjects   ❑ reading   ❑ math   ❑ social studies

❑ English   ❑ science   ❑ spelling   ❑ computer literacy

❑ health   ❑ vocational   ❑ fine arts   ❑ physical education

❑ other _____

4. *List the subject areas from number 3 in which the student needs additional assistance from special education to further develop competencies leading to mastery. Also list appropriate, effective teaching methods from number 2 above, which would lead to more competent performance:

Subject   **Effective Teaching Methods**

The point of IEPs should be to gather information that develops into direction. Explanations of problems tell us only what's wrong and what's not working. Exceptions tell us where to go and what works. In the same way that directions for a new gadget tell us how to assemble the parts, special education meetings might include new ideas based on what already works with a student, no matter how minimal his or her competencies may seem. This direction will assist teachers, administrators, and parents alike to focus on the student's competencies instead of deficits, and encourages goodwill and systemic collaboration between parents and students.

"Something Good Is Happening at School"

When I taught junior high school in the 1970s, I recall a teacher suggesting at a faculty meeting that parents needed to hear good news from school. She came up with the idea of "Something Good Is Happening at School" notes. She suggested that we give them to students who pass their science tests or perform well in choir, band, or football. I liked this idea and sent out my share of notes. What was especially important is that the notes made the teachers the experts in determining what was good. Educators know how class should be held and assignments completed, but I have to wonder what would have happened if a different kind of note was given to the student and the parent:

SOMETHING AMAZING IS HAPPENING AT SCHOOL!

Dear Susie and parent,

I have noticed something interesting about Susie recently. She has taken a renewed interest in her science work and is now passing all her subjects! We are delighted here at Concord Junior High and amazed at her self-motivation. Congratulations!

Mrs. Jones

Pitfalls and Safeguards: When Confused, Imagine

"Typically, in school consultation, the teacher comes with a concern. Often it is about a child or young person who is causing concern because of his/her learning or social behavior" (Ajmal & Rees, 2001, p. 155). The concern is something the teacher wishes she did not have and wants to fix. By employing the assumptions of solution-focused thinking, teachers are led into conversations about resources, goals and exceptions. "The idea that change can occur is promoted through imagining, pretending and experimenting" (Ajmal & Rees, 2001, p. 155).

After the training begins, whenever you see teachers trying out the solution-focused process, compliment them with curiosity in your voice and language such as, "Wow! How did you know to do that?" This genuine compliment goes further than praise because it suggests that they are experts. Remember that you want them, not you, to be the experts. That promotes and maintains change when school clients begin believing in themselves. The same language that is useful with students works with teachers, administrators, staff members, and parents. It can be contagious.

Action Plan: Start with the Students

This chapter has presented ideas for pulling the solution-focused program together. But it's only the beginning. Within the walls of your school are numerous ways for integrating the solution-focused process. Begin by listing the programs and activities of your guidance program. Then integrate questions, forms, and thinking that keep competency in the forefront. The results will certainly turn out to be exceptional.

Bibliography and References

Ajmal, Y., & Rees, I. (2001). *Solutions in schools.* London: BT Press.

Berg, I. K., & Miller, S. D. (1992). *Working with the problem drinker: A solution focused approach.* New York: Norton.

Berg, I., & Steiner, T. (2003). *Children's solution work.* New York: Norton.

Davis, T., & Osborn, C. (2000). *The solution focused school counselor.* New York: Brunner-Routledge.

de Shazer, S. (1985). *Keys to solutions in brief therapy.* New York: Norton.

de Shazer, S. (1988). *Clues: Investigating solutions in brief therapy.* New York: Norton.

de Shazer, S. (1991). *Putting difference to work.* New York: Norton.

de Shazer, S. (1994). *Words were originally magic.* New York: Norton.

Dolan, Y. (1991). *Resolving sexual abuse.* New York: Norton.

Durrant, M. (1993). *Creative strategies for school problems.* New York: Norton.

Epston, D., Freeman, J., & Lobovits, D. (1997). *Playful approaches to serious problems.* New York: Norton.

Epston, D., & White, M. (1990). *Narrative means to therapeutic ends.* New York: Norton.

Franklin, C. & Streeter, C. (2003). *Solution-focused alternatives for education: An evaluation of Gonzalo Garza Independence High School.* Austin: University of Texas at Austin, School of Social Work.

Furman, B. (2004). *Kids' skills.* Australia: St. Luke's Innovative Resources.

Metcalf, L. (1994, 2008). *Counseling toward solutions.* Hoboken, NJ: Wiley.

Metcalf, L. (1998). *Solution focused group therapy.* New York: Free Press.

Metcalf, L. (2003). *Teaching toward solutions.* New York: Crown House Publishing.

Metcalf, L. (2004). *The miracle question.* Bancyfelin, UK: Crown House Publishing.

Metcalf, L., & Chilton, S. (1994). *PALS for life.* Waco, TX: American Red Cross.

Myerhoff, B. (1982). Life history among the elderly: Performance, visibility and remembering. In J. Ruby (Ed.), *A crack in the mirror: Reflexive perspectives in anthropology.* Philadelphia: University of Pennsylvania Press.

O'Hanlon, W., & Bertolini, R. (Eds.) (1999). *Evolving possibilities: Selected papers.* New York: Bruner Mazell.

O'Hanlon, W., & Weiner-Davis, M. (1989). *In search of solutions.* New York: Norton.

Thompson, M. (2002). *Can narrative therapy heal the school "family"?* National Association of Independent Schools. Washington, DC.

U.S. Department of Education, www.ed.gov.

White, M. (1988). *Saying hullo again: The incorporation of the lost relationship in the resolution of grief: Collected papers.* Adelaide, South Australia: Dulwich Centre Publications.

Winslade, J. M., & Monk, G. D. (2006). *Narrative counseling in schools* (2nd ed.) Thousand Oaks, CA: Sage.

Index

A

Abuse, 85–87

Action plans: for elementary schools, 30–31; overview of, 12; to reduce special education referrals, 69–70; for secondary schools, 31–32; for support groups, 94–95; and teamwork, 52

Administrators: gaining support from, 7–9; in referral process, 63; role of, in change, 14; solution-focused strategies implementation by, 60–61; and training issues, 52

Ajmal, Y., 117

Alternative schools: gaining buy-in from, 31; successful examples of, 97–100

ARD meetings, 112

Art, 83

Assessment. *See* Evaluation

B

Behavior modification approaches, 101

Behavior, positive. *See* Positive behaviors

Blame, 105, 108

Buy-in, of staff, 7–9, 69, 79

Buy-In Questions worksheet, 7–9

C

Cadell, J., 83–84

Certificates, for teachers, 11, 41

Change: administrator's role in, 14; and assumptions of solution-focused approach, 62; difficulties of, 11–12; and principles of solution-focused programs, 23–24; and referred students, 103–104; training tips for, 30

Cleaver, E., ix

Code of honor, 98–99

Collaboration, 63

Communities, 1

Competencies, 44

Conversations: case studies related to, 54; implementation of, 60–61; in referral process, 64–67; special education referral worksheets related to, 56–57

Coping skills, 73

Counseling Toward Solutions (Metcalf), 61

Counselors: in referral process, 63; role of, in group therapy, 76–78; role of, in solution-focused school, 9–10

Curriculum, 88, 89

D

Davenport Community Schools, 58, 61, 68

De Shazer, S., 15–16, 78

Depression, 13

Drawing, 83

E

Einstein, A., 1

Elementary school teachers, 30–31

Elizabeth II, 13

Empathy, 49

Epston, D., 82, 105–106

Evaluation: of referred students, 103–105; of school, 2–6; and solution-focused process, 62, 63

Exceptions, 68; and assumptions of solution-focused strategy, 62; and IEPs, 117; and parent conferences, 108–109; and support groups, 73, 74, 76, 77

Expectations, of students, 68

Externalization, of problems: in group therapy, 82–84; training exercise for, 27–28

F

Families, school staff as, 13–14, 30. *See also* Parents

504 plan, 51

Franklin, C., 98–100

G

Garza Independence High School, 97–100

Generic process groups, 84–85

Gibran, K., 97

Goal setting: and group therapy, 74–75, 77, 78; and principles of solution-focused programs, 22; process of, 15; and team cooperation, 49

Group counseling. *See* Support groups

Guide Sheet for Parent Conferences, 110–111

H

Healing groups, 85–87
Helpful Steps That Create a Solution-Focused Direction handout, 16, 18–19
Hooker, C., 43–45, 46

I

Individual Diary form, 78–80
Individualized Education Plan (IEP), 112–117
Individuals with Disabilities Education Act (IDEA), 68
Information gathering: from parents, 108; from students, 106–108
In-service meetings, 10–11

L

Labels, 22, 72, 81
Language: in group therapy, 92; during parent conferences, 108–109; and solution-focused assumptions, 62; and solution-focused process, 63, 68; training exercise about, 26
Least restrictive environment, 62, 68
Legislation, 68
Listening, 49

M

McNew, A., 88
Mean Girls (film), 73–74
Mentor Program Student Information Sheet, 32, 39
Mentor Program student letter, 38
Mentor Program Student Survey, 37
Mentors: gaining staff support for, 32; matching students to, 32; problems encountered when implementing, 12; in solution-focused versus problem-focused school, 1
Metcalf, L., x, 61, 77
Miracle questions, 90
Miracle Worker Referral Form, 33
Miracle Workers Conversation Script, 34–36
Mississippi Bend Area Education Agency, 58, 61–67
Monk, G. D., 10
Morale, 60
Motivation, 77

N

Narrative Counseling in Schools (Monk & Winslade), 10
Narrative Means to Therapeutic Ends (Epston), 105–106
Narrative therapy, ix
No Child Left Behind Act (NCLB), 68
Note writing: to encourage student-teacher relationships, 105–106; to share good news, 117; training exercise about, 28–29

P

Paradigm shift, 2
Parent conferences, 103, 108–111
Parent Consent for Group Counseling form, 93
Parental Consent form, 92
Parents: as experts on their children, 49–50; and federal legislation, 68; meeting needs of, 51; sharing good news with, 117; in solution-focused versus problem-focused school, 1; support groups for, 88–89
Parent-Teacher Association, 32
Past problems, 75
Patience, 51–52
Peers, 68
Peter, L. J., 53
Positive behaviors: and principles of solution-focused programs, 24; sharing good news about, 117; and teacher referral form, 103; team identification of, 46; and wraparound programs, 44
Principals. *See* Administrators
Problem solving, teachers', 12, 16
Problems, cause of, 22

Q

Questions: for administrator buy-in, 7–9; to discover school's purpose, 14–15; in group therapy, 81, 82–84, 85–87; in program implementation, 11, 12; and solution-focused assumptions, 62. *See also* Scaling questions

R

Rebellion, 103
Redescribing behavior, 26, 52
Rees, I., 117

Referrals: action plan for, 69–70; case studies related to, 53–55; and elementary school training, 30–31; overview of, 58; and solution-focused assumptions, 62; and solution-focused implementation, 69; and solution-focused mindset, 59–60; and solution-focused model, 62–63; and solution-focused philosophy, 62; and solution-focused process, 63–67; for special education students versus challenged students, 58; and strategy implementation, 61; for student-teacher conflicts, 101–103; worksheets related to, 56–57

Relationships, student-teacher, 99–100

Resistance, to change, 103

Rewards, for teachers, 11, 15, 41

Ripple effect: and group therapy, 78; and principles of solution-focused programs, 22–23; in teams, 46

S

Scaling questions: in group therapy, 75, 84; training exercise about, 26–27. *See also* Questions

School: climate of, 13–14, 101; discovering purpose of, 14–15; evaluation of, 2–6; problem-focused versus solution-focused, 1

School Strategies Survey, 2–6

Secondary school teachers, 31–32

Self-esteem, 100

Shannon, N. L., 49–50

showyourlogo.com, 32

Simplicity, of solutions, 90

Solution Focused Group Therapy (Metcalf), 77

Solution-Focused Ideas to Remember handouts, 21–25

Solution-focused programs: benefits of, 7; description of, 62–63; history of, 15–16; implementation of, 10–12, 14, 60–61, 69; principles of, 21–25; versus problem-focused programs, 1–2, 15–19; process of, 63

Special education referrals. *See* Referrals

Special education students, 58

Staff meetings, 1

Streeter, C., 98–100

Student Information Sheet, 106–107

Student-teacher relationships, 99–100, 105–106

Support groups: action plan for, 94–95; basic guidelines for, 88–92; beginning of, 94; challenges of, 94; counselor's role in, 76–78; externalizing problems in, 82–84; format for, 89; generic, 84–85; for healing, 85–87; implementation of, 90; meeting times for, 82; member tracking sheet for, 87; naming of, 81–82; overview of, 87; parental consent for, 93; for parents, 88–89; theme of, 78–80; topics of, 71–72

Support services, for students, 63

Surveys, 2–6, 37, 38

Suspensions, 49

T

Task assignments: and parent conferences, 109; and support groups, 77; for teams, 46

Teacher Observation Sheet: Alternative School Success form, 32, 40

Teacher Referral Form, 101–102, 112

Teacher Suggestions for Group Counseling handout, 90–91

Teachers: and expectations of solution-focused programs, 68; and federal legislation, 68; gaining support from, 20, 31–32; implementation concerns of, 69; in-service meetings with, 10–11; and mindset toward special education, 59–60; in referral process, 63; referrals from, for student-teacher conflicts, 101–103; rewards for, 11, 15, 41; in solution-focused versus problem-focused school, 1–2; students' relationships with, 98–99, 105–106; in successful alternative school, 98

Team Summary of Exceptions worksheet, 46, 48

Teams, of teachers: case studies related to, 44–45; cooperation among, 49; goal setting of, 49; growth of, 45–46; maintaining patience with, 52; meetings of, 46–48; negative statements from, 45; venting of, 49

Teamwork, 14

Theme, of group therapy, 78–80

Thompson, M., 13

Time: and group therapy, 75, 82; and principles of solution-focused programs, 24, 25

Training, staff: at elementary schools, 30–31; exercises for, 15–29; overview of, 15; patience with, 51–52; pitfalls of, 30; at secondary schools, 31–32

Trauma, 85–87

U

U.S. Department of Education, 68

V

Violence, 51–52

Volunteers, 32

W

Walkup, T., 78, 81

White, M., 82

Winslade, J. M., 10

Wood, W. A., 43

Worldview, students', 23

Wraparound facilitators, 43–45

Counseling Towards Solutions Workshops

The ideas in this book are available as workshops and can be presented to school counselors, teachers, staff members, social workers, school psychologists, therapists, and more. All workshops are presented by Linda Metcalf, Ph.D., and can include the following agenda:

1. Introduction to the solution-focused approach and its usefulness in a variety of school settings, processes, and programs.

2. Guiding solution-focused ideas and their direct application to a variety of school issues, explained with the use of many case studies.

3. Application of solution-ocused ideas to school issues such as discipline, classroom management, parent conferences, special education/IEP development, teacher-student relationships, parent-school relationships, and more.

4. Explanation of narrative therapy and its application to school issues: how to externalize problems so that the student becomes empowered and the school staff sees beyond the pathology, toward the strengths of students who are challenging.

5. Specific ways to work with adolescents to rebuild reputations, and how to use the miracle question and story writing to assist elementary school students see themselves differently. Additional ideas for helping students bothered by depression, anger, sexual abuse or trauma are provided.

All workshops are very interactive, utilizing brief lecture, motion-picture excerpts, videos of actual cases, role-play exercises, and planning exercises.

To schedule a solution-focused workshop for your staff, please contact:

Linda Metcalf, Ph.D.
5126 Bridgewater
Arlington, TX 76017
(817) 690-2229
dr_linda@ix.netcom.com